A STORM
TOO SOON

A STORM
TOO SOON

A REMARKABLE TRUE SURVIVAL
STORY IN 80-FOOT SEAS

MICHAEL J. TOUGIAS

Christy Ottaviano Books

Henry Holt and Company

New York

Henry Holt and Company, LLC
Publishers since 1866
175 Fifth Avenue, New York, New York 10010
mackids.com

Henry Holt® is a registered trademark of Henry Holt and Company, LLC.

Library of Congress Cataloging-in-Publication Data is available.
ISBN 978-1-62779-281-3

Our books may be purchased in bulk for promotional, educational, or business
use. Please contact your local bookseller or the Macmillan Corporate and
Premium Sales Department at (800) 221-7945 ext. 5442 or by e-mail at
MacmillanSpecialMarkets@macmillan.com.

First Edition—2016 / Designed by Liz Dresner
Printed in the United States of America by R. R. Donnelley & Sons Company,
Harrisonburg, Virginia

10 9 8 7 6 5 4 3 2 1

To Dorothy Aufiero and Luke Wiedeman,

two special people who inspire me

CONTENTS

INTRODUCTION
SAILORS AND RESCUERS

Seventy-foot waves batter a tattered life raft 250 miles out to sea in one of the world's most dangerous places, the Gulf Stream. Hanging on to the raft are three men: a Canadian, a Brit, and their captain, JP deLutz, a dual citizen of the United States and France. The storm sank their sailboat, and now the waves repeatedly toss the men out of their tiny vessel. The captain, JP, with nine broken ribs, is hypothermic and on the verge of death. However, he is a tough-minded character, having survived a difficult childhood; now he must rely on those same inner resources to outlast the storm.

Trying to reach these survivors before it's too late are four Coast Guardsmen battling hurricane-force winds in their Jayhawk helicopter. Once they commit to the rescue, they find themselves in almost as much trouble as the survivors, facing several life-and-death decisions, with the rescue swimmer in an emergency situation. Here is their thrilling story.

SAILORS

Jean Pierre de Lutz ("JP")
Rudy Snel
Ben Tye

JP   RUDY   BEN

RESCUERS

Jayhawk Helicopter Crew

Nevada Smith (Aircraft Commander)

Aaron Nelson (Copilot)

Scott Higgins (Flight Mechanic)

Drew Dazzo (Rescue Swimmer)

C-130 Search Plane Pilots

Paul Beavis (Aircraft Commander)

Edward Ahlstrand (Copilot)

Search and Rescue (SAR) Coordinator

Brian Avelsgard

PART I

FLORIDA—COUNTDOWN TO THE CROSSING

The flight from Ottawa to Florida is a long one, but Rudy Snel doesn't mind as he gazes out the aircraft window at the clouds below. He's thinking about the next leg of his trip: a voyage on the *Sean Seamour II*, a forty-four-foot sailboat that will carry him and two others from Florida to France. Sailing across the Atlantic has been a dream of Rudy's since he was nine, when his family emigrated from the Netherlands to Canada, crossing the Atlantic on a passenger ship. In the course of the voyage, they encountered a storm that caused the ocean liner to pitch and roll, making just about everyone on board seasick. But not Rudy. He was out on the top deck in the pelting rain having the time of his life, awed by the raging sea around him.

Rudy is now sixty-two years old and recently retired from a teaching career in the public schools. He finally has the time to live out his dream of returning to the sea. A Canadian with gray hair and a neatly trimmed beard, he is an adventurous soul; the hardships expected on a transatlantic crossing don't bother him in the least. He owns his own sailboat and often sails the Ottawa River, but he has also mastered piloting small aircraft and parachuting. He has made more than six hundred parachute jumps. On one of those jumps, his parachute did not deploy properly. He looked up at the tangled mess during his free fall but never panicked. Instead, he calmly deployed his reserve parachute and landed safely. His reaction wasn't one of alarm but one of annoyance.

When he saw a notice on a website announcing that a crew was needed for a transatlantic crossing, he immediately contacted the captain. Rudy explained that he wanted to go on the voyage to learn about offshore sailing and most especially because it would be an entirely new experience.

~

When the plane touches down in Jacksonville, Florida, Rudy disembarks and follows the crowd down to baggage claim. He is met by the captain, fifty-seven-year-old Jean Pierre de Lutz, who goes by the nickname JP. The two men shake hands and then head outside. The warm, humid air embraces Rudy, a welcome change from the cold of Ottawa. It is late April, the temperature is in the mid-eighties, and the sunshine causes Rudy to squint.

They drive directly to the *Sean Seamour II*, which is moored at Green Cove Springs on the St. Johns River. Rudy likes what he sees. The sailboat has a center cockpit protected by a hard dodger (rigid windshield), a single mast directly in front of the cockpit, and twin guardrails surrounding the white vessel. During inclement weather, the cockpit can be completely enclosed with canvas curtains and windows. It's a sleek-looking boat—Rudy thinks it's beautiful.

The third crew member, Ben Tye, emerges from the boat's cabin. JP introduces the thirty-one-year-old sailor to Rudy. Ben is British, with a short, stocky build and a shaved head. He began his career in the tourism industry, but he soon turned his interest to the sea, teaching inshore sailing on small vessels. He has sailed from Europe to the United States, and on this trip he will reverse course. Reserved by nature, Ben tends to take time before opening up. But that night at dinner, he already feels comfortable and is more than satisfied that the threesome will make a good crew. He's impressed that JP has spared no expense in equipping the boat and is taking his time readying it for the crossing. In his quiet manner, JP patiently explains the intricacies of his vessel, and Ben senses that this is a man who never gets rattled.

Ben and Rudy don't know it, but JP had more than a dozen

candidates answer his request for a crew. He interviewed each applicant, narrowing them down to two crew members, relying on his instincts to determine who would be the best fit. He was more than sure that Rudy and Ben were the right men for the job. JP selected May as the optimal time of year for an eastbound crossing of the Atlantic, primarily because it would put them ahead of hurricane season. He'd had a brush with a hurricane in a prior crossing and wanted no part of another.

The voyage is not scheduled for another few days because the *Sean Seamour II* was in storage for two and a half years and needs a complete overhaul, cleaning, and provisioning. Some of the equipment was removed and stored in an air-conditioned warehouse. Now that equipment needs to be inspected, replaced if necessary, and secured in its proper position aboard the boat. Rudy and Ben will work under JP's supervision.

The preparation introduces Ben and Rudy to the inner workings of the boat as they replace lines, clean equipment, and practice using the pumps. The two men lay out the drogues (pieces of fabric that can be trailed behind the boat to add stability during storms) on the dock.

A vital piece of equipment on any boat is a radio beacon, which can signal to land that the boat and crew are in distress. These beacons are crucial in the telling of this rescue, and the two kinds referred to throughout the book are:

- GPIRB—global position indicating radio beacon, which can send a signal to the Coast Guard quickly pinpointing the location of an emergency
- EPIRB—emergency position indicating radio beacon, an older piece of equipment that sends a signal but does not use GPS technology

The life raft and the GPIRB went out for recertification, and the entire crew now reviews their operation before securing the two pieces of safety equipment. In addition to the GPIRB mounted in its cradle inside the cabin of the *Sean Seamour II*, there is also an older EPIRB from an earlier boat of JP's on board. Although it is a somewhat redundant piece of equipment, JP has tested its eleven-year-old batteries and the unit works, so he decides to keep it on board. He installs the EPIRB in its cradle on the inside of the cockpit's dodger, where it's safe from sea spray. The EPIRB is water-activated, and the captain doesn't want any false alarms.

JP reviews the heavy-weather contingencies with the crew, making sure they understand exactly what needs to be fastened down in a storm. They examine the location and operation of all safety equipment. One person will be on watch at all times, and they will all wear safety harnesses with tethers clipped to the boat at night and in heavy weather. The tethers are six-foot-long lines: if a man falls overboard, he will not get swept away from the vessel and can try to climb back on board.

The time spent working on the boat has been valuable for the three sailors to get to know one another before heading out to the open water. Rudy is glad for the few days of preparation; if he found anything of concern about his crewmates, he figured he could always back out of the voyage. He knows a transatlantic crossing has its risks, and he wants to feel extra comfortable with his partners. They will be in close quarters for several weeks. Rudy has a good feeling about both men. Ben is a knowledgeable sailor and a fun companion, and JP is soft-spoken, easygoing, and competent.

Departure is scheduled for May 1, 2007, but the men have to wait an extra day for some new batteries. This one-day delay will have significant consequences.

JEAN PIERRE

B efore beginning the voyage at six thirty in the morning on May 2, JP checks the marine weather forecast and finds nothing out of the ordinary. As the three men untie the lines, some friends from the marina come down to wave good-bye. JP then makes good on a promise. He will stop smoking now that the voyage has begun. To prove it, the short and slender captain with wispy gray hair takes his last pack of cigarettes, ceremoniously holds it high in the air, and tosses it into the water—his new life as a nonsmoker begins at this moment. Rudy and Ben exchange glances. They hope their relaxed captain doesn't turn into Ahab, the angry captain featured in the classic novel *Moby-Dick*.

Using the motor, JP guides the *Sean Seamour II* down the

St. Johns River, going right through the heart of Jacksonville, Florida, as the sun clears the eastern horizon. As the boat approaches the first bridge, Rudy can't help but wonder if the mast—all sixty-one feet of it—will clear the underside, but JP assures him it will, and it does. Near the river's mouth, they stop at a marina to top off the diesel tanks and fill up spare containers with more fuel. During the refueling, Rudy walks to a market and purchases three orders of fish and chips.

JP uses this opportunity to call his wife, Mayke (pronounced *My-keh*), a successful artist. They talk for a few moments, but JP wonders why Mayke is so mad at him for not calling earlier. She doesn't tell him the real reason: She has had an uneasy feeling that the voyage will not go well.

Mayke knows her husband is a safety-conscious sailor and that the *Sean Seamour II* is more than capable of handling rough weather. But ever since she dropped JP at the airport a couple of weeks earlier, her apprehension has grown in intensity with each passing day. Sleep has been difficult, and her time painting in the studio has suffered. She just wants her conversation with JP to end before she blurts out her misgivings and puts a damper on his enthusiasm for the voyage.

~

When Rudy returns with the fish and chips, the men enjoy their lunch—their last meal from the outside world. Then they resume motoring, reaching the ocean at two p.m.

I'm finally doing it, thinks Rudy as he watches the shore disappear. *We're on our way.*

There's a slight breeze from the southwest, and the men are able to get their sails up. They're at the edge of the Gulf Stream, a current in the ocean that runs from the tip of Florida northeast along the coast of the United States. The Gulf Stream's current will help propel the *Sean Seamour II* northeastward on the early days of the journey. Their plan is to sail northeast toward Bermuda and then turn due east toward Europe.

After watching the sunset, JP and Ben go to bed while Rudy stands watch to make sure they don't get too close to any other vessels. He is assisted by a radar unit that will sound an alarm if another vessel is in the vicinity. Rudy wears his safety harness with the tether clipped to a firm object on the boat. This precaution is especially wise at night because a sailor who goes overboard in the dark has a slim chance of being found. There are few fates worse than swimming frantically and hollering in the darkness, trying to keep up with a boat whose stern lights are growing fainter and fainter.

Rudy's glad he has the first watch; he's much too excited to sleep, and he's already thinking ahead to tomorrow, his first full day at sea. Just before midnight, with a half-moon illuminating the water, Rudy has his first thrill of the trip. He's startled by a splash a couple of feet away from the boat. Peering at the ocean, he sees the outline of a dolphin come through the water. There are perhaps twenty dolphins swimming along either side of the *Sean Seamour II*, occasionally breaking the surface with acrobatic leaps. Rudy watches, mesmerized. He has never seen dolphins at sea, and this pod seems to want to race the boat, just a few feet away from the awestruck Canadian. Grinning, Rudy feels a sense of well-being from contact with the natural world of the sea.

Looking from the radar screen back to the dolphins, Rudy expects the pod to veer away from the boat at any moment. Instead, the dolphins accompany the sailor for the next hour. Finally, at about one a.m., the dolphins leave, and Rudy checks a computer navigation screen that shows both the actual course of the sailboat and the course plotted in advance by JP. The vessel seems a bit off track. Rudy decides to wake JP and get his advice.

JP joins Rudy in the cockpit, and together they get the boat back on course and sail into the night. JP loves sailing so much, he doesn't want to miss any of it by sleeping. Like many die-hard sailors, he has had an unconventional life. JP was born in New York City to a French father and a Belgian mother. They were not ready to raise a child, and JP's father was abusive to both his son and his wife. Because of the ill treatment, JP's mother fled her husband, abandoning her three-year-old son. Neighbors often heard him crying and called social services when they realized he was left alone for hours at a time in his father's apartment.

Social services removed JP from the apartment and placed

him in a foster home, which was little better than his lonely existence in the apartment. He was the youngest of several children there, and the older boys bullied him. But he was a resourceful child, and out of necessity he adapted, learning that he could survive by being alone and hiding when necessary.

When he was six years old, JP's father somehow managed to regain custody of him. JP went to live with his father and his new wife, Betty. The following years were disastrous for young Jean Pierre because his father was both physically and verbally abusive. His stepmother, Betty, was a kind woman, but she, too, had to flee the cruelties of her husband when JP was ten years old, leaving him alone with his father. In an effort to get his second wife back, JP's father concocted a heinous plan. Knowing Betty loved the boy, he surmised that if she realized JP was in trouble, she would return.

In an unspeakable act of cruelty, his father intentionally dropped boiling water on his son. The "accident" accomplished his father's intended effect: Betty returned out of concern for the boy. She, too, was a victim of this manipulative madman.

Shortly after JP's recovery, Betty arranged for him to be reunited with his biological mother, wanting to get him away from her husband. JP was shipped off yet again, this time to France, where his mother lived by the ocean. The young boy, who had endured so much cruelty, found that the sea had a soothing effect. Saint-Tropez, on France's Mediterranean coast, opened JP's eyes to the marvels of the ocean. When he wasn't in school, he spent much of his free time prowling the seawalls while expectantly watching the fishing boats come and go from the port.

Soon the local fishermen noticed the quiet American boy watching them, and one kindly fisherman finally motioned for JP to come aboard his boat. The fisherman explained that if JP arrived at the wharf early the next morning, he could join the man on his fishing trip. That began several years of JP's quest to learn everything he could about the ocean and boats.

~

JP's aspiration was further fueled when he read about the exploits of sixteen-year-old Robin Lee Graham, who set out to sail around the world in his twenty-four-foot sloop named *Dove*. *National Geographic* published periodic articles of the young sailor's adventures as he sailed through the South Pacific, was demasted twice during storms, and met his future wife on the island of Fiji. It took Graham a little over four years to complete his journey, but nevertheless, when he finished in 1970, he became the youngest person to sail solo around the planet. Graham became JP's inspiration and hero.

JP thought the adventure of circumnavigating the world was the perfect challenge, and he vowed that someday he would set sail and not return until he had crossed the seven seas. Neither JP nor Graham minded being alone, but there was one big difference in their childhood: Graham had a loving father who had taught his son to sail and celebrated his son's independent streak. JP didn't let his past slow him down; he simply taught himself what he needed to know or asked questions of his fisherman friends.

JP's dreams of blue-water sailing were put on hold when he was seventeen and attended landlocked Syracuse University in New York, then later found a job in Germany. The young man had a sharp mind that could intuitively solve problems. He also had a pair of hands that could make or fix just about anything. In 1978, he put those talents to use, starting his own business developing and marketing consumer products, including toys and household goods. Four years later, he sold the business.

JP had married and fathered three children when new business opportunities prompted him and his family to move from Europe to the Washington, D.C., area. His heavy workload and frequent travel kept him not only from the sea but also from his family. Soon his marriage fractured, ending in divorce in 1995.

After the divorce, JP turned his attention back to the sea, often walking the harbors and boatyards, eyeing different models of sailboats. He purchased a thirty-three-foot sailboat that he christened the *Lou Pantai*, which roughly translates to "The Dream" in an old dialect that was spoken in the Provence region of France. Living aboard the *Lou Pantai* where it was moored at Annapolis, Maryland, JP planned his blue-water voyage. He read every sailing book he could find to help him prepare the vessel for a transatlantic crossing. JP was a loner by nature, and that cold winter, while living solo aboard his vessel, he felt exhilarated by the possibilities that stretched before him.

In 1996, JP began his long-awaited transatlantic trip. The first leg of the voyage took him to Cape Cod, Massachusetts, to visit his stepmother, Betty. He set sail from Annapolis on July 4, reaching the Cape a few days later. JP was ecstatic to be out on the open sea, feeling much as he did as a boy during that first trip on the fishing boat from Saint-Tropez.

Once moored at Cape Cod, JP had to wait for Hurricane Bertha to pass by, up the East Coast. When the storm had spun its way north of Massachusetts, he monitored the weather forecasts and decided he could set off safely for Europe. Betty went down to Harwich Port to see her stepson off with hugs, kisses, and more than a few tears.

JP thought Hurricane Bertha was long gone, but the storm had a surprise for both meteorologists and the lone sailor. Four days into the voyage, while in the Gulf Stream, JP ran into building seas. Bertha, now downgraded to a tropical storm, had not continued north after reaching the Maine coast but instead had veered east-southeast and into the path of the *Lou Pantai*. The winds increased to over fifty knots, and the waves climbed to twenty-five feet. (A knot is a nautical unit of speed equal to 1.15 miles per hour.) Realizing he could not stay at the helm all night, he decided to deploy a drogue (fabric that drags like a parachute) to keep the vessel's drift to a minimum. But as he prepared this equipment, an extreme wave spun the sailboat completely around, causing the slack in the line attached to the drogue to tangle in the propeller.

Battered by crashing waves, the *Lou Pantai* rocked so violently that JP had difficulty moving without being thrown to the deck. Water infiltrated the engine tank vents, and the boat lost power. The wind screamed through the rigging, fraying JP's nerves, making him feel as if he were inside a screeching violin. Somehow he made it through the night without being injured, but during the next day and evening, the waves grew to thirty feet. JP's sole source of comfort was the knowledge that he had an emergency beacon called an EPIRB on board. Later that night, the seas became so chaotic that he considered activating the EPIRB, but he forced himself to hold back, not wanting to put rescuers in danger. He had made up his mind he would not call for help until the boat was actually sinking.

During the desperate hours, he wrote a good-bye letter to each of his three children, telling them how much he loved them. When the notes were written, he sealed them in bottles and tossed them overboard.

Through the long and terrifying night, the wallowing *Lou Pantai* somehow remained afloat, and when dawn finally came, the winds abated a bit, and JP knew the seas would follow. Later that day, when the waves became manageable, JP tied a line around his waist and entered the water with a mask and snorkel. Over a five-hour period, he worked on cutting the sea anchor line from the propeller and shaft. When the job was done, the bruised and exhausted sailor resumed heading eastward.

The rest of the three-week voyage was without incident, and JP felt an enormous sense of gratitude and accomplishment. He had not only completed his transatlantic crossing but survived the worst conditions that the ocean could throw at him. Or so he thought at the time.

3

RIDING THE GULF STREAM

May 3 is another fine day, and with a brisk breeze from the west, the *Sean Seamour II* is now traveling north-northeast, riding the current of the Gulf Stream. Rudy is surprised by the change in the ocean's color, from a greenish-gray hue to a brilliant aquamarine, and he marvels at the sun's ability to shine right through the top of small waves. He also notes that the ocean's temperature has climbed from the previous day's seventy-three degrees Fahrenheit to seventy-eight today.

The warm waters of the Gulf Stream are a result of its origination in the Gulf of Mexico. Its current shoots through the fifty-mile-wide Florida Straits, passing between the tip of

Florida and Cuba, sending the flow northward along Florida's eastern seaboard. Here the Gulf Stream is narrow, deep, and quick-moving, just like a high-speed river in a well-defined path. It is approximately forty miles wide, a quarter mile deep, and traveling at a clip of four to five knots. This beginning section of the Gulf Stream carries a volume of water more than twenty-five times as great as all the rivers in the world combined. When it reaches Cape Hatteras, it curves to the northeast, losing a bit of its power as more warm-water eddies detach and re-form, while the Stream itself broadens and slows. Most of the warm-water eddies spin north out of the core of the Gulf Stream, rotating in a clockwise current, and some of these separate completely, spinning off on their own meandering paths.

Farther north, the Gulf Stream flows eastward, forming the North Atlantic Drift, slowly heading across the Atlantic and ultimately traveling past the British Isles. Although its temperatures are not as warm there as they are off Florida, the Gulf Stream still moderates the climate off Western Europe and is said to be the reason why palm trees grow on the southern end of Great Britain.

The Gulf Stream presents challenges for sailors. Its waters warm the air directly above it, helping to produce a microclimate. Sailors can often see the location of this saltwater river long before they arrive. Low clouds may hover above the Gulf Stream, owing to rising warm air and water vapor. If the warm air collides with a cold front, violent thunderstorms erupt, with severe localized wind, rain, lightning, and even the occasional waterspout. Yet forecasting when these thunderstorms will occur is difficult because of how quickly they form.

Even worse than the thunderstorms are existing weather systems that intensify above the Gulf Stream when they feed off the warm ocean below. Tropical storms passing over the Stream can explode into full-fledged hurricanes, and sailors are especially wary during the height of hurricane season, in late August and September. In addition, the Gulf Stream is not the place to be caught in a storm due to the size of the waves that can occur.

When winds come out of the northeast, they produce waves surging toward the southwest, and these waves become larger and steeper when they run into the Gulf Stream's current flowing in the opposite direction. Steep waves mean breaking waves, and these avalanching combers can cause havoc to boats. Some sailors would rather face a swell twice as big as a cresting wave simply because the swell slides under the boat, while the breaking part of a wave can engulf it in the churning water. And if a wave spins a boat completely around so that it comes down the face of a wave bow-first, the ultimate disaster can occur: the vessel can pitchpole. This happens when the bow is buried in the trough, or valley, and the stern is picked up by the surging sea and hurled over the bow, capsizing the boat.

JP is aware of the advantages and the potential dangers of voyaging along the Gulf Stream—yet another reason he chose the beginning of May to set sail. He knows he will be well beyond Bermuda by June 1, the start of hurricane season. Several other sailboats are also in the Gulf Stream, making their annual voyage from the southern U.S. and Caribbean toward the cooler climates of ports from Maryland to Maine.

~

That afternoon Ben surprises his crew members with an English custom by serving them tea. A little later, Rudy prepares dinner (the men will take turns), and as on the previous day, they take advantage of the fine weather by eating in the open air of the cockpit.

The cockpit features a seat for the helmsman (who steers the boat) behind the wheel and cushioned benches for passengers. Just aft (behind) the cockpit is the canister that contains the six-person Zodiac Bombard offshore life raft. From the cockpit, there are three steps down the companionway (staircase) that leads to the main salon or cabin. The chart table and communications center are to starboard (the right), while on the port side (the left) are the dining table and a wraparound bench.

As the men eat dinner, JP mentions that the latest weather report continues to call for favorable conditions. Rudy can't remember when he last felt so relaxed. No phone calls, no television, and no schedules. Even the sunset looks as stunning as any he's ever seen, with shades of pink, red, and orange shining over the dark sea below. A bit later, when it's completely dark, he sees his first phosphorescence. The strange light is caused by the chemical reactions in bioluminescent plankton. Because earlier mariners incorrectly thought the shimmering light was the mineral phosphorus, the term *phosphorescence* is sometimes used for the phenomenon of the glowing plankton. Its beauty is enhanced by the waves, moving the plankton and causing the light to be bright one minute and less so the next. Some sailors think the radiant light looks like millions of stars or an aurora borealis (also known as the northern lights). Rudy just thinks it's beautiful.

The entire trip so far has been magical for Rudy: the dolphins, the changes provided by the Gulf Stream, and now the shimmering sea. Ben and JP have seen these marvels on their prior trips, but observing Rudy's astonishment makes them feel the wonder anew. The *Sean Seamour II* is sailing smartly, and in the distance they see the lights of a large ship passing by and the light from a nearby weather buoy.

As the men enjoy the night, Rudy asks JP how he came to own the *Sean Seamour II*. JP smiles and thinks, *Where to begin?* He explains that after he crossed the Atlantic in his first boat, the *Lou Pantai*, he devoted the next couple of years to actively managing his inn in France while increasing its size by six guest rooms. It was during this period that he met Mayke, and their relationship blossomed during trips on the *Lou Pantai*. They eventually replaced the *Lou Pantai* with the *Sean Seamour I*, soon to be followed by the larger *Sean Seamour II*. JP had learned much on his earlier Atlantic crossing and felt the *Sean*

Seamour II—a heavier boat with a center cockpit—would be ideal for his ultimate goal of circumnavigating the globe. The name *Sean Seamour* was chosen by Mayke and is a play on Jean Pierre's first name and his love of the sea: *sea* and *amour* (which means "love" in French).

In 2006, JP and Mayke purchased a home in a remote hillside village thirty miles north of Saint-Tropez, France. At the time, the *Sean Seamour II* was in Florida, and in 2007, JP started to make plans to bring the boat back to France. That's how this current voyage came about. JP ended his conversation with Rudy by telling him that for the first time in his life he felt fully content. He had a wonderful wife, a home in the hills, and the sailboat he'd always dreamed of.

SPIRITS ARE HIGH

May 4 is another sunny day, but with little wind, the crew of the *Sean Seamour II* relies on the boat's motor to propel them northward. JP senses a change in the weather pattern and carefully analyzes the latest updates, but he discerns nothing ominous. As the morning progresses into afternoon, the temperature climbs, and Rudy announces that he's going for a swim. Ben and JP look at him as if he's lost his mind, but Rudy says he's serious. JP kills the engine, and the boat comes to a stop.

Rudy dives into the sea from a small platform at the stern of the boat. As he surfaces with water streaming off his gray beard, he beckons for the others to join him. Rudy's got a smile from ear to ear; it's clear he absolutely loves taking a swim so many miles out to sea.

Ben and JP stand on the deck scrutinizing their crewmate as he breaststrokes around the sailboat. He doesn't look cold. It's obvious Rudy is truly enjoying himself. Within a minute, the two men dive in and join their friend, invigorated by the water, which, while not quite bath temperature, is still pleasant enough.

None of the men express concern about sharks, although the Gulf Stream has its fair share, from migrating great whites to prowling makos that can grow to thirteen feet in length. The mako is the more aggressive of the two and can reach speeds of up to thirty-five miles per hour. "Shark hunter" anglers have seen hooked makos leap out of the water almost twenty feet in the air, and more than one mako has then turned and attacked the boat where the anglers stood in disbelief.

Sharks can sense vibrations in the water from long distances, and on this calm day, the movement of the swimming men would be easy to detect. The sailors know there are sharks close to shore as well as offshore, but 99 percent of the time the sharks avoid humans. JP gives them little thought, because he has never been bothered by the predators of the sea in his many years of diving and snorkeling.

Sharks are not the only large predators in the Gulf Stream. Yellowfin tuna, mahimahi, and blue marlin all hunt there as part of the food chain that starts with plankton and progresses up through various sizes of bait fish and on to the bigger fish.

Writers from Zane Grey to Ernest Hemingway have told tales of epic angling battles with large fish in the Gulf Stream, and that is what JP has in mind after his crew safely completes the swim.

After sunning himself for a few minutes on deck, JP goes below and comes back with a fishing rod and a brightly colored lure. He restarts the boat's motor and trolls the lure fifty yards behind the vessel. The afternoon passes quietly, and the fish don't bite, so the men decide to try their luck tomorrow.

~

May 5 begins as a quiet morning, and the *Sean Seamour II* continues northward under motor power rather than sails. JP works on equipment, Ben catches up on reading in his berth (bedroom), and Rudy mans the cockpit, looking out over the endless expanse of calm blue ocean. The fishing rod is set in the rod holder, and its line trails far behind the boat. A small bell hangs near the tip of the rod so that if no one is paying attention and a fish strikes the lure, the men will hear the tinkling bell as the rod tip jerks toward the sea.

Around midday, Rudy sees his first flying fish. He is astonished by just how far it can leap, using its winglike pectoral fins to glide over the ocean's surface. The flying fish he watches cover well over seventy-five feet in a straight trajectory with little arch. They burst from the water using their tails to power them upward, usually to escape predators. Some schools have been clocked doing close to forty miles per hour and traveling more than a thousand feet at a height of twenty feet above the water.

In the afternoon, Ben is on deck and hears the bell on the fishing rod ring. He springs up and grabs the rod, which is arched over at an almost ninety-degree angle. Something large has grabbed the lure, and Ben hollers to his crewmates that a fish is on the line.

Ben, Rudy, and JP take turns with the rod, cranking the reel, putting all their strength into bringing the catch closer to the boat. They have no idea what is on the other end; although the fish is fighting hard, it never jumps. Ben grabs a gaff (a large hook to lift the fish) and waits by the stern. Finally, after a twenty-minute fight, the three men get a good look at the fish. It's a mahimahi, and they whoop with joy, knowing what a fine-tasting fish it is.

Also known as the dolphinfish, mahimahi (the name is Hawaiian for "strong strong") is a beautifully colored creature with an iridescent gold-and-blue body and a strange-looking head. Instead of the top of the head tapering gently toward the mouth, as with most fish, the male mahimahi's head is rounded, and the female's head is almost flat. While most mahimahi average three to six pounds and are a couple of feet long, they can grow as long as five feet.

The mahimahi JP is now fighting appears to be a big one, and he carefully guides it toward where Ben is crouched with the gaff. Ben reaches down, lets the point of the gaff get under the fish, and then yanks it up with both hands, and the prize is on the deck. The mahimahi is almost four feet in length and weighs a solid twenty-five pounds: enough meat for dinner and many fillets for the freezer.

Before Ben and JP begin to fillet the fish on the stern deck, JP reminds Rudy to make sure all the portholes in his cabin are shut, as Rudy's berth is directly below where they will be cleaning the fish and washing the deck down. Rudy goes below and closes his hatches but somehow misses the one right over his bunk. Sure enough, when JP later pours buckets of seawater over the deck to wash off the fish blood, some of it goes right into the open porthole below. The men have a good laugh later when Rudy comes up from below, saying his cabin smells like fish.

The sailors enjoy dinner on the open deck. It's another evening in a warm paradise as the western sky turns shades of purple and pink. JP stares toward the setting sun longer than the others and observes that the western edge of the Gulf Stream appears to be clouding up. After the meal, he downloads weather reports for the second time that day but again notes that the two low-pressure systems and the two high-pressure systems spread out over the western Atlantic are in about the same positions. The forecast does not call for any storms in their vicinity, so JP keeps the boat on the current course but a wary eye on the clouds to the west.

That night, during Rudy's watch, high, thin clouds occasionally block out the moon and stars, and the night is as black as obsidian. When a break in the clouds occurs, the stars seem to overflow from the opening, and Rudy feels as if he can almost reach out and grab one. Random thoughts flow through his mind like the drifting clouds above. He's glad he decided to retire early from his position as a vice president with his local teachers' federation, allowing time for this voyage. He thinks of his father and two friends who died before they had a chance to do the things they planned for retirement.

~

Later that night, when JP comes up to relieve Rudy of his watch, the captain says he thinks it prudent to adjust their course. The squall lines on the western edge of the Gulf Stream are moving east, and the latest weather report shows the two low-pressure systems moving a bit closer. JP explains that if heavy weather is to hit, he wants to be out of the Gulf Stream. They will exit the Stream by heading east. He wants to play it safe.

Near dawn, Ben enters the cockpit to relieve JP of watch. The skipper uses the break to download the latest weather information, which predicts that in the next few hours, the winds will reach twenty to thirty-five knots and come out of the north. JP shares the news with Ben, and the two sailors agree that the change in course is the right move. Ben jokes that Rudy might get his wish and be able to sail through a patch of rough weather.

The change in the weather does have one benefit: the men can get the sails up and move along at a good clip. Spirits are high, and the sailors enjoy a bracing ride that increases to seven knots. Even if the wind does reach thirty-five knots, both Ben and JP have sailed through far stronger, and they are exhilarated rather than fearful as the *Sean Seamour II* plows evenly through the still-calm ocean.

THE GATHERING STORM

That same day, at JP's hillside home in France, his wife, Mayke, begins her daily hike with her two dogs up to their mountaintop perch. She and the dogs climb up a rough dirt road littered with rocks. They pass ancient chestnut trees rising from enormous gnarled trunks, and finally into the high country of low shrubs, where wild boars live.

Mayke wonders how JP is faring on his voyage and how far up the Gulf Stream he might be. Since he left on the trip, her days have been agonizingly slow, and painting has been difficult. The subject of each of Mayke's paintings is never planned out—she lets her hands guide her, and images begin to take form. Her last painting was of a woman sitting alone, staring at an open door.

It takes her a bit longer than usual to reach the summit because she hasn't been sleeping well from being on edge, worrying about JP. These climbs to the hilltop usually relax her, but not today. When she reaches the mountaintop, she sits down and gazes across the hazy valley. After a few minutes, her heart starts racing, and the landscape she is staring at is replaced by a vision. She sees the inside of a boat, dark except for a few dim and flickering lights glowing from various pieces of electronic equipment. The cabin is moving violently, first up and down and then yawing from side to side. Her heart beats faster. *What is this?* she asks herself, feeling alarmed and nauseated. Her eyes are open, and she is not asleep, not dreaming.

Then, as suddenly as the vision came, it is gone, and before her are the green hills stretching off toward blue skies. She wishes she could tell JP to abort the trip and sail to the closest port, but he is far from cell phone range. She doesn't know there are no ports near the current position of the *Sean Seamour II*. The vessel is approximately 240 miles off Cape Hatteras, North Carolina, and 400 miles from Bermuda.

~

Across the ocean at about dawn, JP is taking over the watch from Rudy. Sitting alone in the cockpit of his boat, JP tries but fails to appreciate another sunrise. His thoughts are fixated on the latest weather report downloaded from the Internet. It shows the low-pressure system to the north of the *Sean Seamour*

II deepening and gathering strength. To the south, the other low-pressure system is moving in a northwesterly direction, slowly closing the gap. Forecasters are calling for winds to increase throughout the day and max out at thirty to thirty-five knots.

JP squints at the horizon and sees an aircraft carrier steaming off his starboard bow far in the distance, likely heading toward Norfolk, Virginia. He raises the carrier on the radio, and the Navy radio operator confirms that their latest weather report is the same as JP's: increasing wind with rain as the low-pressure system intensifies. JP thanks the operator and continues to sail east, away from both systems and the potential hazards of the Gulf Stream.

Later in the morning, Ben and Rudy are in the cockpit, thankful for the great speed they are making away from the Stream. The waves are four feet high and choppy, but the *Sean Seamour II* slices through them at seven and a half knots. This is the kind of sailing Rudy had hoped for. The invigorating breeze, salt air, and steady progress of the boat make him feel completely alive.

At one p.m., the two men notice wispy yellow-brown clouds to the north.

"What do you make of those clouds?" asks Rudy, keeping his eyes fixed northward.

"Rain is coming, and maybe a squall," answers Ben.

Rudy nods. "I don't think I've ever seen clouds that color. They're so menacing."

JP comes up from below, glances toward the stained clouds, and says, "The winds are forecast to veer out of the north to northeast late in the day, and that's when they are supposed to really pick up. We're in for some rough weather, so let's prepare."

The three sailors discuss the approaching weather and decide they don't want to get caught with too much sail up. If the wind suddenly picks up to extreme force, it will be dangerous to get the sails down. They begin lowering the sails but continue advancing toward the east and away from the Gulf Stream.

An hour later, the winds are howling at forty-five knots out of the north-northwest. Raindrops, propelled horizontally by the wind, lash at the three sailors. JP thinks, *This is not good. Nothing is going as planned. The weather is not as predicted.*

Even though they are almost fifty miles east of the Gulf Stream, it still influences the gray seas around them because they are at the edge of a large eddy that has extended outward from the Stream. The seas are chaotic, and waves have grown to ten to fifteen feet. JP reefs (lowers and rolls) the remaining sails and then raises a small portion of a storm jib sail meant to stabilize the vessel. The progress of the *Sean Seamour II* has slowed considerably, and cold rain pours from the angry sky. All three men put on their safety harnesses and tether themselves to the boat.

Rudy has long since stopped reveling in the boat's bracing ride and is becoming increasingly concerned about the wind, which seems to get stronger by the minute.

As the afternoon wears on with no letup from the storm, JP considers his options. His original plan to sail north of Bermuda later that night no longer looks feasible with the diminished headway. Making a run to Norfolk is out of the question because they would have to cross the Gulf Stream, and besides, they are much too far out to sea to beat the storm to land. The storm is already happening.

JP checks the latest weather reports, but they are the same, forecasting maximum winds of thirty-five knots. *Well,* he thinks, *I learned from Hurricane Bertha to expect the unexpected.* And this is the unexpected: JP is soon clocking gusts of up to sixty knots that cause the *Sean Seamour II* to pitch and roll, which makes moving about increasingly difficult. He decides that the best course of action is to reverse course and ride with the storm rather than try to make headway against the wind. Even with the anticipated wind shift out of the north-northwest to the north-northeast, he has plenty of sea room to run and still avoid the Gulf Stream. He also decides to lay his largest drogue off the stern. The drogue is a wise choice, since it acts as a drag on the boat, counteracting the wind and waves that push the boat forward. The drogue device looks like a parachute with holes on its side. Trailed at the end of a long line, it can be a lifesaver. Besides slowing the *Sean Seamour II*, it also helps stabilize the boat.

Ben and Rudy assist JP, feeding the drogue line through the main winch on the port side. JP crawls to the stern of the vessel and guides the line through the starboard stern cleat.

Despite the heaving of the boat, JP has no trouble balancing while he works. For a fifty-seven-year-old man, he is nimble, and his motions are quick and efficient—almost catlike. The men set out three hundred feet of line and feel it is the right amount, because the *Sean Seamour II* is riding the waves with greater stability.

Ben has weathered storms at sea before, and he thinks this one is manageable, particularly now that the drogue is set. The wind seems to read his thoughts. A powerful gust blasts down on the men and pries Ben's tight-fitting wool cap right off his head, flinging it into the sea.

The three sailors go below, secure the companionway hatch behind them, and seal themselves in the belly of the boat. The *Sean Seamour II* is battened down, and all the men can do is wait for the winds to blow themselves out.

Daylight gives way to evening, and the storm shows no signs of abating; in fact, it is increasing in power. The snarling waves are twenty feet, and many are steep enough to break, filling the ocean with white water and streaks of foam. Each time a comber hits the hull, the entire boat shudders, and occasionally a larger wave slams the vessel with frightening power. More than one wave smacks so hard that Rudy likens it to being hit by a truck. *Good God,* he thinks, *that felt more like a solid object than liquid.* The three men glance at one another, but nobody says anything. They know they are in the grip of a major storm, and the only thing between them and the hungry ocean is the fiberglass hull of their vessel.

Around eight p.m., Rudy's curiosity gets the best of him. He takes a couple of steps up the companionway, partially slides back the hatch, and peers into the darkness. He is immediately greeted by stinging pellets of water that feel like tiny needles being stuck into his face. Cupping his hands around his eyes, he can see enormous black walls of water towering menacingly above the boat. It's a terrifying sight, and Rudy estimates that the waves are over thirty feet. The roar of the wind and crashing seas is deafening. He has seen and heard enough and ducks his head, seals the hatch, and climbs below, telling the others about the size of the waves.

Rudy sits at the navigation station, keeping one hand on the seat and the other on the bulkhead to steady himself as the boat's motion becomes more and more erratic. Ben is wedged in tight at the salon, but JP can't seem to sit still. He's fidgeting and constantly checking instruments, his brow lined with concern.

Rudy checks the anemometer (wind gauge) and can't believe his eyes. Whenever the boat rides up out of the trough, they are assaulted by seventy- to eighty-knot winds, with frequent gusts of eighty-five. He turns toward the others and shouts out the wind speed. JP is stunned. He knew it was bad out there, but eighty-five knots is crazy. He didn't even know his anemometer could measure anything beyond eighty. The storm is exploding so fast it is hard to believe.

JP doesn't say anything, though he can't help thinking this is like 1996 (when he was mauled by Hurricane Bertha) all over again. But this time he knows the storm is even worse. He hopes the *Sean Seamour II*, a larger boat than his *Lou Pantai*, can withstand the punishment. Bertha almost killed him, and he knows he is in for a long night. This time around, he feels the added pressure of responsibility for Ben and Rudy. He hopes his silence does not betray his anguish for the extra burden he carries. Whatever this freak storm is, JP has a hunch that it's just getting started.

The storm pounding the *Sean Seamour II* also has another nearby sailboat in its clutches. The *Flying Colours* is caught off guard by the sudden ferocity of this quick-forming storm. Meteorologists, too, are surprised by the storm's behavior. Unlike many low-pressure systems that travel from the tropics or Africa and then expand when they reach the Gulf Stream, this storm began at the Stream, in the same region where the *Sean Seamour II* is being battered. The two minor low-pressure systems that JP was tracking earlier in the day pulled together to form one supercell that deepened so rapidly that no meteorologist could have predicted its power.

Adding to the storm's surprising characteristics, it does not travel up the coast, as most storms do, but instead wobbles in place and then ever so slowly drifts to the southeast. A strong high-pressure system to the north has blocked its path, ensuring that its fury will have plenty of time to generate mammoth waves.

Meteorologists call such a storm a bombogenesis because of how abruptly it forms and explodes. They will later label this early stage of the storm as an extra-tropical cyclone that will evolve into subtropical storm Andrea. But the sailors caught in the storm know only that they are being lashed by hurricane-force winds, and it doesn't matter that the "official" start of hurricane season is three weeks away. And the worst part is that there is not a darn thing they can do about it except sit tight, keep vigilant, and wait.

HELP IS GREATLY NEEDED

As the hour approaches midnight, the average wave size has increased to an incredible fifty feet, and the *Sean Seamour II* is carried up the face of each swell until it teeters at the very top and slips down the back side. Occasionally, a wave crests and breaks so that as the boat begins to rise, the comber cascades directly on it, jarring the men's bodies and their nerves as the sailboat takes the blow.

They all know that one wave can engulf the boat and just about anything can happen. The vessel might be knocked on its side until it rights itself in the trough, or it could be knocked down and continue to roll 180 degrees in a complete capsizing. An even worse, but very real, scenario could occur if the drogue fails or is snapped free; the vessel might surf down an especially steep wave so fast that the bow would be buried in the trough and the stern picked up by the wave and pitched directly over the bow. This pitchpoling is so violent that a sailboat capsized in this manner could suffer severe structural damage and never recover, as hundreds of gallons of water flood the interior. Should the sailboat stay in one piece, passengers would likely be severely injured.

Ben is aware of these possibilities, and as he hears the occasional breaking seas outside the hull, he knows these fifty-foot mountains of water are pushing the limits of the *Sean Seamour II*. He has always known that blue-water sailing has its share of risks, and should he sail for a lifetime, he figured he'd eventually encounter danger. He just didn't expect it to come so soon in his sailing career.

Rudy's luck is even worse—here he is, on his very first sailboat voyage on the ocean, and he's in the maw of a monster storm. He is not dwelling on his misfortune but instead is listening to the chaos outside. When the vessel takes a direct hit from a wave, the boat groans, and Rudy feels it vibrate at the top of the wave, where the shrieking wind and churning water can fully attack the *Sean Seamour II*. He breathes a sigh of relief when the surging water passes and the vessel is in the eerie silence of the trough. Then the next wave comes, and the same terrible sensations begin again. The analogy to being on a roller coaster is an accurate one, particularly when the coaster approaches the top of the incline, where it always slows before plunging down, picking up speed all the while. It's that sense of hesitation and then of free fall, if only for a split second, that is so unnerving.

The waves are probing and jabbing the boat for weakness, ready to pounce if they should find any. Rudy can't help thinking that the *Sean Seamour II* is in the hands of a raging giant who is shaking and then punching the boat, trying to get inside. Every now and then the sea—the giant—seems to relax a bit, as if gathering strength for the next onslaught.

Rudy is exhausted by the cumulative effect of the lurching boat, the loud thuds on the hull, and of not knowing how much worse it will get. The uncertainty of what lies ahead makes it nearly impossible to relax. The waiting seems interminable, and he feels as though he's been in the storm for two days rather than a few hours.

~

It's just after midnight, and May 6—one of the longest days of the three men's lives—is behind them. They wonder what May 7 will bring. Rudy eats a couple of granola bars for energy, offering some to JP and Ben, then decides that if he doesn't at least try to get some rest, he will be too fatigued to be useful when the storm abates. His nerves are frayed, and his muscles tired and cramped from sitting by the chart table and tensing up each time a wave pounds the hull. He suspects the two other men feel the same, even though no one has said a word for the last half hour.

JP encourages Ben and Rudy to get some rest. Ben thinks, *This is worse than being held captive. We can't fight back in any way.* He's right—there are no more precautions they can take, and even if they think of one, it's too dangerous to go topside. It's all up to the boat. Every screw, rivet, line, seam, and porthole, as well as the rest of what makes up a sailboat, has to hold under the assault of the seas.

Ben lies down on the port bench where he has been sitting, folds his arms across his chest, and closes his eyes. Rudy lurches to the rear cabin and lies down on the bed. JP continues to sit at the chart table. It is now approximately one a.m.

Five minutes later, there is a thunderous boom. In that second, Rudy goes from resting in his bed to being airborne, hurled across his cabin and into the bulkhead, hurting his back. In the salon, Ben, too, is thrown into the air, traveling from the port side toward the chart table, where JP is sitting. To JP, it seems as if time has transitioned into slow motion. He can see Ben's arms and legs flailing, coming sideways through the air. JP instinctively raises his hands to protect himself, and in the next split second, Ben barrels into him. One of JP's hands makes contact with the back of Ben's head, and the other pushes his shoulders, deflecting Ben ever so slightly so that the two bodies avoid a bone-breaking collision. Ben is turned so that his back and buttocks hit the bulkhead where the TV is mounted; it shatters in a spray of glass and plastic.

All this happens in the first second of the furious impact of a rogue wave. In the next second the damage continues, sending the *Sean Seamour II* careening over on its starboard side. Objects not bolted down are hurled through the boat like missiles, and canned soft drinks burst like rockets, spraying in all directions. Almost as abruptly as the vessel was knocked down, it springs back up, and the loose objects roll to the opposite side of the cabin.

The men don't know it, but the force of the wave was so great that it snapped the drogue trailing behind the boat. There is nothing to slow the boat as the angry seas have their way with it.

$\sim$

Rudy and JP half walk, half crawl to Ben and help him up. He is bruised from being launched through the air, but he insists he's okay. JP's gaze sweeps through the galley and salon. He notes that while everything is in shambles, there doesn't seem to be any seawater pouring in.

"What happened?" shouts Rudy. So much adrenaline is going through him that he forgets about the pain in his back.

"It was a knockdown!" hollers JP. "I've got to check the deck, got to see how bad things are!" He doesn't say that he thinks the boat totally capsized, rolling a complete 180 degrees.

JP is dressed in his yellow foul-weather gear and has on an uninflated yellow life jacket that is part of his safety harness. Ben and Rudy are dressed the same way, except Ben's foul-weather gear is red.

JP climbs the companionway, pausing for a second at the top. *Think everything through. Nothing rash.* Carefully, he slides back the hatch. Pellets of spray pepper his face and sting his eyes. The volume from the wind roaring and the waves crashing sends a jolt of fear down his spine. Amazingly, the deck light is shining, and he can see that the mast is intact. Then his eyes widen as if he's been slapped in the face by an unseen hand. He realizes the entire hardtop dodger is gone. The older EPIRB from his previous vessel was mounted on its cradle and attached to the dodger, and of course that has been swept away as well. It does not have a hydrostatic (water-active) release, so he assumes it sank with the heavy fiberglass dodger before it had a chance to transmit. Turning aft, he squints in the gloom and notices a wonderful sight: the container with the life raft in it is firmly secured to the vessel.

A wave breaks over the stern, soaking JP and sending water cascading down the companionway. There is nothing more he can do, so he ducks down and seals the hatch. A million thoughts are racing through his mind. *We've had a capsizing, and we are hundreds of miles from help. We likely have structural damage.*

I'm responsible for the safety of Ben and Rudy. What will happen if an even bigger wave hits the boat? He realizes there is a good chance the vessel will be so damaged that it won't right itself, or if it does, it will still eventually sink. Even if the boat stays afloat and survives the storm, he reckons the damage will be such that the vessel will be adrift and in peril.

Ben and Rudy are staring at JP, waiting for him to speak. "The hard dodger is gone. I don't know what other damage there is, but we have the life raft. We're going to need help no matter what happens, so I'm activating the GPIRB. Once they get the signal, the Coast Guard will get the info about the boat and call us on the satellite phone, and we can let them know what's happening."

JP figures that if the phone won't work, at least the Coast Guard will know there is a boat in trouble and can follow its location as it drifts. He is certain the Coast Guard knows about the hurricane-force winds, and he concludes that the conditions will prohibit any rescue by helicopter. *But at least they'll know where we are and will come as soon as they can.* And help is greatly needed. JP can sense that the vessel is not as stable as before and is taking more broadside hits, and he knows there is likely more damage than he could see when topside.

Rudy and Ben agree with the decision to set off the GPIRB. Ben has been in a storm during a previous transatlantic crossing, but nothing like this, and no knockdown. Hearing about the damage topside only confirms his feeling that the storm is overwhelming the boat's equipment. *At some point soon,* he thinks, *we've got a good chance of getting hit by another monster wave, and then it may be too late to call for help.*

Rudy is not only worried about the vessel; he's also concerned that one of the crew may be injured. *It's a miracle no one is seriously hurt from being thrown across the boat. We need help. And we also need a little luck. We've got to make it to daylight. Everything will be better then.*

JP activates the GPIRB, and its small strobe light blinks, as does the light that indicates the unit is transmitting. There is relief on the *Sean Seamour II.* The Coast Guard will know that there are three souls in distress.

~

The knockdown of a vessel by a wave is a larger version of a beachgoer being hit in the surf by a wave that happens to break exactly where the person is standing. It's almost impossible to stay upright when the full force of the wave collapses on you. The *Sean Seamour II* has stayed upright for several hours despite being walloped by waves that grew to fifty feet, with the occasional fifty-five-footer in the mix. Incredibly, these waves are bigger than the vessel, and it's a testimony to its construction that it rode on through the night as long as it did. For the most part, the waves slid underneath the boat. The loud thuds—the sound of water impacting against the hull—were the waves with crests that slammed against the vessel, staggering it until the wave continued its onward slide beneath the vessel. The wave that knocked the boat down was a bit different. It was likely sixty feet in height. As the comber lifted the *Sean Seamour II* out of the trough, it, too, began its slide beneath the keel. But the wave was so large, so steep, it could not support itself and probably started breaking halfway up its face, with the full force of the water not just slamming the hull but engulfing it. Like the beachgoer in heavy surf, the *Sean Seamour II* didn't stand a chance. The initial impact—the kinetic force of it—sent Ben and Rudy flying and then pushed the vessel down the face of the wave, where the following surge completed the capsizing.

The design of the sailboat, particularly its lack of large windows, was one reason the knockdown was not more catastrophic. In countless Coast Guard marine casualty reports, the trouble on either a sailboat or a powerboat starts with a window or porthole. Most of these structures are made of Plexiglas and usually the weakest points on a vessel. Windows slanted by the deck near the bow, rather than on the sides of the boat, are the most vulnerable in a storm; there, breaking waves plunge directly down on the vessel. The sheer force and weight of the wave—just one cubic yard of water weighs nearly a ton—dropping on a window will either break the window or loosen its mounting, making the next wave more likely to shatter it completely. Storm shutters can reinforce the window, but they must be installed before the trouble begins.

Once a window has been breached and water floods the

boat, succeeding waves will carry more water inside. Then the fight begins. Bilge pumps may become clogged with debris and shut down or be unable to keep up with the water. Crew members frantically bail with buckets, pots, pans, or whatever they can find, and they must dump that water out the broken window or out the companionway hatch, neither of which is a good option in a storm.

The three men on the *Sean Seamour II* don't have any shattered windows to worry about—yet. Their focus is on the storm, whose magnitude was predicted by no one. They simply can't believe it is still raging, and they are trying not to dwell on whether or not it has peaked. They know that if the last rogue wave had been a few feet larger, they may not have survived. And with the drogue severed from the vessel, it is mostly riding the waves beam-on and occasionally surfing down some liquid cliffs at unchecked speeds.

PART II

7

MULTIPLE MAYDAYS— THE SAR COMMAND CENTER

A lthough it's the graveyard shift, Search and Rescue (SAR) Coordinator Brian Avelsgard is wide awake and busy at the Command Center in Portsmouth, Virginia. Two other coordinators are working alongside him, and they also have called their captain, David McBride, at home and woken him up to keep him apprised of the rapidly changing situation. Each of these coordinators has a computer with a dual monitor, a couple of phones, and an assortment of emergency procedure manuals for different scenarios. The computers are used for rescue planning. Coordinators can input the type of vessel (particularly the amount of freeboard exposed to the wind), the estimated flight time for a C-130 plane to reach the boat in distress, and current on-scene weather. The computer then assists the coordinator in determining where the vessel may have drifted by the time the aircraft arrives.

The SAR team is well aware that the low-pressure system has grown to a powerful storm centered approximately two hundred miles out to sea off the coast of the Carolinas. The prior evening, when the storm's leading edge first impacted the inshore waters, the coordinators worked a case involving three fishermen on an eighteen-foot powerboat. The captain of the vessel had radioed the Coast Guard at eight p.m., explaining that he and his friends were trapped in a salt marsh due to wind and waves overpowering the boat. Brian Avelsgard dispatched a small Coast Guard utility boat to rescue the crew, but the rescue attempt had to be aborted because the water in the marsh was not deep enough for the utility boat. The only way to get the men off the vessel was by helicopter, so one was dispatched at nine p.m. The rescue swimmer faced an unusual challenge. Instead of being dropped into the ocean, he was lowered into three feet of water with a mud bottom and performed the rescue while standing up. All three fishermen were hoisted up without incident.

Although the rescue sounds like a simple one, Avelsgard was relieved when it was over. Anytime he sends a helicopter up at night, he knows the challenges to the crew are doubled. Now he must be aware that the helicopter crew has used up some of their flying hours. Crews have "bag limits," or maximum flight times that must be monitored to make sure they have some rest before logging too many hours. Exhaustion is as dangerous to flight personnel as weather conditions are.

Now, at approximately two a.m., Avelsgard is keeping track of the sailing vessel *Seeker*, which is dragging anchor off Diamond Shoals. He has been in communication with Coast Guard Station Oregon Inlet, whose radio operator is in contact with the sailboat captain. They are hoping that the boat can remain in deep water until daybreak, when a rescue won't be as dangerous. The captain agrees that he is not in a Mayday situation and that he will keep the Coast Guard advised of his situation with periodic updates.

Suddenly, an EPIRB distress notification flashes on the SAR Center's designated computer screen. It is not from the *Seeker* but from a vessel named the *Lou Pantai*. Coordinator Avelsgard has no way of knowing that this is the name of JP's earlier boat, indicating that the signal came from JP's backup EPIRB. It washed off the *Sean Seamour II* during its knockdown and came free of the hardtop dodger so that it floated on the ocean and transmitted. (This is a minor miracle because it does not have a hydrostatic release mechanism to free it from its cradle. It should have sunk with the hardtop dodger.) At this point, there is no location associated with the beacon. Avelsgard will have to wait for another satellite to pass before he can get a fix, and this length of time can vary widely from case to case. In the meantime, Avelsgard reviews the telephone contacts that the owner of the EPIRB listed when the device was first registered. By making these calls, the SAR Center can gather a wealth of preliminary information. First and foremost, coordinators hope they can talk to the captain of the vessel so they can find out if the EPIRB is a false alarm or truly a distress signal.

While Avelsgard is dialing the number for the first contact associated with the *Lou Pantai,* yet another distress signal comes in. This one is from a GPIRB registered to a boat named the *Cold Duck.* A fixed location is given at approximately 225 nautical miles southeast of Elizabeth City, North Carolina, on the eastern side of the Gulf Stream, near the center of the storm. One of the coordinators starts to call the *Cold Duck*'s contacts, beginning with the home telephone number of the boat's captain, located in Alabama. The coordinator expects the captain's wife or a family member to answer and confirm that the vessel is out on the Atlantic and that the distress signal must be for real. Instead, the captain himself answers and says he is at home in bed. He explains that his boat is safely moored at a harbor on the Alabama coast and that the GPIRB must be malfunctioning or that someone tampered with it. The coordinator asks him to go down to the boat and disable the GPIRB so they don't get any more signals.

What no one knows is that the identification number for the *Cold Duck*'s GPIRB is the same as the number assigned to the GPIRB that JP bought for the *Sean Seamour II.* The IDs are designated by the manufacturer, and it's up to the GPIRB's owner to fill out the forms that go to the National Oceanic and Atmospheric Administration (NOAA). Both JP and the *Cold Duck* owner did so correctly. JP's GPIRB was the older of the two, so he was the first one to send his information in. Months later, when the *Cold Duck* owner did the same thing, NOAA's clerical process showed that the ID number had been registered earlier. The NOAA operator overrode JP's earlier registration, because each beacon is required to have a unique ID. The operator assumed that there was only one GPIRB and that it had been sold by the owner of the *Sean Seamour II* to the owner of the *Cold Duck,* so the registration for the *Cold Duck* became the active one. The whole GPIRB issue could have been catastrophic if JP had not kept the older EPIRB.

When an EPIRB is activated, a satellite detects the signal and relays the information to a NOAA group called Mission Control, located in Maryland. The operators at Mission Control decode the satellite information and convert it to longitude and latitude to determine which Coast Guard SAR Center is closest to the accident scene. The location fix, along with the identity of the vessel in distress, is passed to the proper SAR Center on a dedicated communication link via computer. This is how Brian Avelsgard was notified of the *Lou Pantai* EPIRB, followed by the *Cold Duck* GPIRB. Brian and his fellow SAR coordinators are focused on the *Lou Pantai* EPIRB (the one that fell off the *Sean Seamour II*), and just as he begins to call the first contact, a satellite gets a fix on the vessel and Mission Control relays the position: 225 nautical miles southeast of

Elizabeth City. Before Avelsgard can process that this is the same position as the *Cold Duck*'s—which they thought was from a malfunctioning GPIRB—yet another EPIRB signal is detected. This one is from the *Flying Colours,* though no location is fixed. "We got another one!" shouts Avelsgard.

Avelsgard and McBride don't need a location to know that the *Flying Colours* is likely off the coast of the Carolinas, where the storm must be exploding with more intensity than forecast. From Avelsgard's perspective, all hell seems to be breaking loose out at sea. He's had three emergency beacons go off in the last hour, and another vessel, the *Seeker,* is in trouble. The SAR coordinators know they are in for a hectic night, and each person digs in and begins the tasks associated with saving lives.

One of the coordinators alerts the Coast Guard captain of a C-130 search plane that they have an EPIRB hit with a fixed location and that he and his crew should prepare the plane and go to the scene. This advance work will take a bit longer than normal because the C-130 that is ready for the mission is at the civilian airport in Norfolk rather than the Coast Guard air station at Elizabeth City. (Strong crosswinds at Elizabeth City made Norfolk a better spot to have the plane waiting in case of an emergency.) The C-130 crew, staying at a hotel in Norfolk, hop in a van and race to the airport.

The closest Coast Guard cutter, the *Tampa,* is diverted from fisheries patrol off the coast of New Jersey to the distress scene of the *Lou Pantai* and the *Flying Colours.* It will not be an easy mission in such brutal, rampaging seas. They don't expect to arrive for twenty-seven bruising hours. The captain of the *Tampa*, Steven A. Banks, likens the beating they take to being inside a 270-foot-long washing machine in the agitation cycle. Trying to operate in that wild motion takes its toll on the crew; many have sustained cuts and bruises as they brace themselves at their various stations. All the Coasties are focused on reaching the distress area as quickly as possible, knowing that sailors might literally be barely hanging on to life.

The telephone calls to the contacts for the *Lou Pantai* are not going well. First JP's son and daughter are contacted, and both tell the Coast Guard that their father sold that boat years ago. They explain that their father has a newer boat, the *Sean Seamour II,* but they don't know if it is still in port outside Jacksonville, Florida, or if JP is even on it. Now the coordinators are really confused. Avelsgard thinks, *This is bizarre. We have one emergency beacon to a vessel called the* Cold Duck *which is in port in Alabama, another to a vessel called the* Lou Pantai *that's registered to a captain who sold it years ago.* Then he realizes both emergency beacons are transmitting from the same location in the Atlantic, near the storm's center. He is certain a boat is in trouble there, and he's glad he alerted the C-130 crew to get ready to launch. He continues down the contacts for the *Lou Pantai* until he reaches a woman named Betty de Lutz, on Cape Cod.

Betty—Jean Pierre's stepmother—is woken from a sound sleep by the ringing of the telephone. "Hello," she answers groggily.

"This is the U.S. Coast Guard calling. Is your son, Jean Pierre de Lutz, on the ocean?"

"Yes," she answers with trepidation.

"We have an emergency beacon registered to him going off. Do you know the name of his boat?"

"I'm not sure."

"Is it the *Lou Pantai*?"

"Well, that was the name of his old boat, but he sold it. He now has a larger boat, but I'm not sure of its name. But if you have an emergency signal, it must be from him."

Avelsgard tells Betty they are preparing to launch a C-130 plane to go to the boat. "We will call you back soon and keep you updated. We have more than one emergency beacon going off."

Betty immediately starts praying for the safety of her son and his crew. She makes tea and sits by the phone, waiting for more information. When the phone rings, she jumps, then picks up the phone, hoping for good news. Instead, the Coast Guard coordinator asks her to tell him everything she knows about JP's proposed voyage. After they talk, Betty thinks of JP and how tough his life has been. She remembers the cruelty of her former husband toward his son and JP's close call with Hurricane Bertha. But she also thinks of his newfound happiness with Mayke and their home in the mountains. *Mayke! I should call Mayke.* She reaches for the phone. *Wait. Don't do it. There's nothing she can do, and this will just terrify her.*

Betty starts cleaning the house to keep busy, though her mind envisions huge black waves on a storm-tossed sea.

THE WAVE

On board the *Sean Seamour II*, the men are recovering from the shock of their capsizing. After activating the GPIRB, JP begins to assess the conditions inside the boat. He checks the portholes, then looks at the mast, where it comes down through the deck to rest on the keel support grid. Both are in good shape. There is some water in the bilge, the lowest section inside the boat, below the floorboards. JP is able to quickly pump it out.

JP asks Ben and Rudy to sit on the floor on the starboard side of the vessel. The waves are beating against the port side, and he takes this precautionary measure so that no one is hurled from port to starboard if another rogue wave bears down on the boat. Checking the instruments, JP sees that the winds are out of the northeast, and he shudders to think what might have happened to the vessel if they were directly inside the Gulf Stream. The wind and waves are moving the boat at a steady clip of six knots toward the south-southwest. Though the Gulf Stream is to their west, JP calculates that they are well removed from it. They are, however, in a massive eddy of water warmed by the Gulf Stream, and there is nothing they can do about it. This eddy has moving current that can increase the size of the waves.

The men have done all they can, so they sit quietly, waiting out the storm. No one can sleep with the wild motion of the boat and the ominous bangs on the hull from breaking waves. As the minutes go by, each man is lost in his own thoughts. JP assumes that the Coast Guard is working with an Amver vessel to come to the *Sean Seamour II*'s rescue.

As the time approaches three a.m., JP makes a rudder adjustment. He wants to keep the port side slightly more exposed to the waves than the stern for better stability in sync with the drogue, which was fed off the stern. The boat does not respond as he expects it to, and he is puzzled by the loss of control. After lurching to a porthole in the galley, he can see that the drogue line is taut and assumes it is still attached, but he wonders about the lack of control. He also wonders why the Coast Guard has not called on the satellite phone. He moves to the chart table, takes a seat, and decides to call the Coast Guard, hoping there is a satellite in reception range.

Before he has time to make the call, the boat starts to roll.

It passes the forty-five-degree mark, and the men hold their breath as their eyes widen in fear and disbelief. For a brief, agonizing second, time seems to stop. They feel that they are carried by some unearthly force as the boat continues to turn beyond the 90-degree mark and their world goes upside down. It's a surreal, sickening feeling, even worse than the first knock-down, because this is happening more slowly, giving them time to realize the pure horror of it all. The lights flicker, and a low rumble gains volume as it comes from beyond the confines of the cabin. The rolling motion accelerates and seemingly defies gravity as objects are hurled from one side of the vessel to the other, crashing upon impact. Rudy and Ben are awkwardly pitched into a tumble as the *Sean Seamour II* does a complete 180-degree roll, caught inside the vortex of the wave. JP also starts to fall but is simultaneously slammed by the heavy salon table that has come free of its legs.

Buckets of green seawater flood into the upside-down sailboat.

The vessel has been struck by a colossal rogue wave that marine experts will later estimate is a minimum of eighty feet tall. It is possible that two waves joined forces to create one mass of energy. However it formed, there is no question about its power as it swallows the *Sean Seamour II*, whose mast is now pointing toward the bottom of the ocean.

JP struggles to breathe. Although his head is above the rising water, he's in excruciating pain and suspects he has broken ribs from the impact of the table. Then he feels the water climb up the back side of his neck and head, followed by silence as his ears submerge. He frantically fights to free himself, but he's pinned by the tabletop. *I'm going to drown inside my own boat!* Every neuron and nerve in his body is firing, and adrenaline courses through his limbs, but he cannot move.

Rudy is prone on the ceiling, which has become the floor of the capsized vessel. It takes him a couple of seconds to process what has happened. A single wall lamp is still on, and the first thing he sees is water shooting through two air vents, as if someone is outside with a fire hose. Then he hears shouts: "Help! Help!" He looks toward the cries and, in the dim light, can see a mess of debris, including the tabletop. The top half of JP's head is barely visible above water.

Ben is also disoriented, but JP's hollering snaps him back to reality, and he heads toward the shouting. With Rudy, he pushes the table off JP and pulls the captain's head and shoulders out of the water. JP winces and groans as sharp pain spreads through his chest; slowly, he gets to his feet.

Almost two feet of water is sloshing about, with more gushing up through the ceiling vents below them. Aside from the incoming water, all is quiet. A couple of minutes go by as each man gathers himself and begins to process what has occurred. Ben is waiting for the vessel to right itself, but nothing happens. One thought races through his mind: *I don't want to die trapped inside. Rather die topside. See the sky one last time.* Rudy is having the same thought, and he stumbles to where the sliding companionway hatch should be. He takes off his personal flotation device (PFD), which hydrostatically inflated, but JP steps toward him, grabs him by the shoulders, and croaks, "Stay here!"

JP manages to ignore the throbbing in his chest. He has one thing on his mind: the life raft. *Is it still with the boat? If the boat doesn't right itself, we're going to need it.* He looks down where the companionway should be and takes a big breath of air. Searing pain shoots through his ribs. Then he lowers himself into the three feet of water and disappears.

Ben and Rudy stare down at the spot where JP submerged himself. A minute goes by and he does not surface. Water sloshes from one side of the vessel to the other, carrying all manner of debris. Rudy kneels down in the water. He sticks his head under and starts to pull his body toward where he believes the companionway hatch should be. He can't see a thing, and he gropes around, trying to feel for either JP or the hatch. He's running out of air and comes back to the surface. He shakes his head at Ben, indicating the futility of his dive. The two men look each other directly in the eye. It is their absolute lowest moment. *Did JP get stuck? Is he drowned? Did the waves take him away?* A creeping panic rises between them, spawned by the feeling that they are entombed. And the water is rising.

～

JP somehow manages to slide open the hatch and swim out, barely able to hold his breath. He needs air, yet he doesn't shoot directly for the surface. Instead, he lets his hands feel their way to the starboard leg of the arch that rises from the stern of the boat, not far from the companionway hatch. He sweeps with his arm, feeling for the life raft canister, and follows the arch to the port side. Still no raft. It should be in the canister just a few inches aft of the arch. His lungs are screaming for air, and he's fighting their call. He can sense that his body will ignore the commands from his brain to hold his breath and that his mouth will open on its own.

Grabbing hold of the toe rail, JP plans to pull himself toward the surface by following the upside-down hull. Suddenly, the boat starts to right itself. It all happens so fast that there is no time to think, and JP holds on as best he can. Incredibly, he lands in a heap in the cockpit next to the helm as the boat rolls out of its capsized position.

Coughing, gagging, and desperately sucking in big gulps of air, the captain is exhausted and disoriented. Five or six seconds go by before he notices a dim light coming from an opening, and he realizes that he's in the cockpit, looking down the companionway steps. The light is coming from the cabin. Hope! The *Sean Seamour II* has something left in her; she's not done yet. A new shot of adrenaline courses through his body, temporarily blocking out the pain of the broken ribs.

Then he remembers that the raft is gone, and his spirits plunge as quickly as they rose. He glances under the arch at an empty space where the raft and canister were mounted on the boat. *Without the raft, we are as good as dead. The boat is on borrowed time.*

The battered captain steals another look down the companionway and realizes the top part of the companionway hatch is gone. He shouts down to Ben and Rudy, "Get the pumps running! I've got to find the raft!"

As JP's eyes adjust to the darkness, he takes a second to collect himself, kneeling in the pulpit area of the cockpit, which is just forward of the wheel. The *Sean Seamour II* is a bit more stable in the raging seas now that it is filled with thousands of pounds of water.

A wave slides beneath the vessel, and when the boat is in the bottom of the canyon, it is eerily quiet, almost serene, giving JP the feeling that he and his crew are the last humans alive on the planet. Then the next wave carries the vessel up to the wind-whipped summit, where his senses are blasted by the roar of breaking seas. With a smudge of moonlight filtering through the cloud cover, he can see the outlines of the mountainous waves and white water at their crests. The sight is so incredible, so unlike anything he's ever seen, that he has to force himself to look away and focus on the boat. That's when he notices that the mast has been cracked, just above deck level, off its base. It is lying off to the port side of the boat, almost parallel to the hull. The lower half of the mast is resting on top of the vessel, and its upper half is in the water. The rigging is a complete mess.

JP squints at the water beneath where the mast is lying. *The raft!* He can't believe it. The raft is fully inflated and pinned against the water by a spreader that extends from the mainmast at a right angle. That the raft wasn't snatched away by the waves borders on the miraculous. But to be able to use the raft, JP will have to remove it from beneath the spreader.

The captain is so determined that for now he is keeping fear at bay. He doesn't stop to think about the fact that he is not tethered to the *Sean Seamour II* and could be thrown off at any second. He inches toward the raft, which appears to be upside down. The ballast bags that normally hang beneath the raft and fill with water for stabilization are on the top, and one of them looks to be pierced by the spreader.

JP has a high tolerance for pain, having experienced severe burns in childhood, but now the adrenaline rush is wearing off, and every movement of the boat causes agony that can't be ignored.

He knows the pain will soon become debilitating. In order to survive, JP must free the raft immediately.

THE LIFE RAFT

J P's resourcefulness seems to be a natural gift, just like that of his hero Robin Lee Graham, on the *Dove*. And like JP, Graham was asleep in his bunk on board the *Dove* when, at two thirty a.m., he heard a rumbling noise and thought his boat had collided with a log or an uncharted reef. He raced topside and found, to his horror, that the mast was broken about six feet up, and most of it was in the water, dragging next to the heaving boat. While sleeping, he had worn his safety harness, but now he had to remove the harness so he could get the mast and the sails back on board. As he struggled with the mast, a large wave slammed the boat. Graham tumbled off the deck and into the sea with no lifeline. It was the first time in his life that he had fallen overboard.

Luckily, the boat wasn't drifting faster than he could swim, and Graham was able to get himself on board. Then, over a two-hour period, he hacked away at the rigging and retrieved the broken mast and sails. When he went into the cabin, he was shivering from the cold. In his book *Dove*, he wrote: "Slowly I began to see that I was in real trouble. Now my muscles ached and I couldn't go to sleep as I thought of the mess I was in. My best chance was a jury rig and hope for good trade winds. Of course, if the winds failed I could drift in this ocean until they found my bones."

The next day Graham cobbled together a small mast and sail, making a second small sail of awning and patching it with a hand towel and a shirt. For the next twenty-four days, he sailed his battered and broken boat until he made landfall and safety.

Perhaps JP's learning about Graham's ingenuity at such a young age rubbed off. From surviving the brutalities of his father to learning to live in a country where he couldn't speak a word of the language, JP endured. Now he would have to do it again.

～

Crouched in the pelting rain and spray, JP is shivering. Because they are in an eddy of the Gulf Stream, the water is relatively warm—sixty-nine degrees—but the wind, out of the northeast, is cold, especially against his wet skin. He squints at the raft on the port side of the sailboat, pinned under the rigging from the fallen mast. Its canopy is torn; it undulates behind the raft with each passing wave. JP fears that if he doesn't get the raft free and secured to the boat quickly, it, too, will tear and deflate in a matter of seconds. He considers calling Ben and Rudy to help him lift the mast and rigging, then realizes that they will have difficulty finding their harnesses and tethers in the mess below. He would never forgive himself if one of the men were swept away from the boat after responding to his request. He sets about trying to free the raft himself.

When a wave rolls beneath the boat, JP notices that the mast rises up a bit higher because the buoyant life raft lifts the rig. He decides to use the waves to his advantage. Because part of the mast is on the poop deck, which is higher than the aft deck, there is a foot of space between the mast and the aft deck.

Crawling on his belly, JP inches his way into the opening. If the mast shifts, he will be trapped.

Lying beneath the mast on his stomach and facing aft, JP is now at the port stern corner of the boat, with the raft only inches away. He reaches out and touches the raft with his right foot; he plans to lift the mast and shove it free of the rigging. With the aid of his left leg, he arches his back and boosts the mast, synchronizing his movement with a passing wave. Piercing pain radiates from his broken ribs, and he cries out as he kicks the raft. It doesn't budge.

Another wave comes and he tries again, but the raft won't

move. He cannot push it far enough to free it from the spreader entangled with the ballast bag.

Panting, he squeezes out from beneath the mast and stares at the raft, knowing he has to somehow cut the bag from the spreader mast. He has shut out the roar of the crashing waves and ignores the drenching he gets when a wave breaks on the vessel. His mind races. *I don't have a knife, and there is no time to get one. The raft is going to rip apart at any minute, and when it loses its air, we are done for.*

He grabs the ballast bag, yanking with all his strength. He can't hear the tear, but he can feel it. He moves his hands farther up the bag and, taking a deep and painful breath, pulls back hard. Again he feels the bag give way. He can see the spreader in its entirety and knows he has freed the bag. Only the weight of the spreader is on the raft. JP slides back into the opening between the mast and the deck. He resumes his position and, with his left leg, pushes the mast upward while shoving the raft with his right leg. At last the raft bobs free of the rigging.

Just as JP begins to lower the mast, an especially large wave breaks directly on him, and the mast is pushed down on the left side of his back, crushing him against the deck. He moans in agony. Although he doesn't know it, another three ribs are broken.

Somehow he is able to inch out from beneath the mast and collapses on the deck, water swirling around his body. The raft is bouncing wildly with each wave. JP knows he must get it starboard for safe boarding.

Fighting through the pain, he forces himself into a crouching position and grabs the tether attached to the raft. He plans to crawl toward the bow, pulling the raft along and then securing it to the opposite side of the boat. A flashback to his sailing accident in Hurricane Bertha gives him pause. He remembers how exposed the bow can be when waves are crashing upon it and how difficult that made it to stay on board. And now, with no safety harness, he realizes that if he leaves the cockpit, he'll likely be swept overboard.

He can't walk the raft around the stern because the protruding mast extends beyond the back of the boat. He decides to lift the raft from one side of the vessel to the other. He tries to pull the raft up, but it is so heavy that it barely moves. Shifting position onto his back, he gets one leg under the raft. Then, pulling with his hands, he is able to get part of it out of the water and on the side railing. Using the waves for leverage, he edges more of the raft out of the water.

A gust of wind catches the raft. The raft comes completely out of the water and flips right over the cockpit, landing upside down on the starboard side. JP, clutching the tether, can't believe his good fortune. He secures the raft to the side of the boat.

Sitting in the cockpit, JP thinks through what should be done next. He wants to wait until the last possible moment to put his crew on the raft. The violence of the waves and the raft's missing canopy mean it will not be an easy ride. *We've got to stay with the boat. We can't leave until I know for sure she is sinking.*

He peers out at the deck, awash in foam and green water, resolving to do whatever he can to keep the *Sean Seamour II* afloat just a little bit longer.

Moving to the companionway, JP can see Rudy and Ben bailing water below in the dim light. He starts down the stairs, ready to tell his crew about the raft. His eyes go to the GPIRB, still in its cradle. He freezes. There is no light from the GPIRB. It is dead.

DESPERATION

Luck. JP, Rudy, and Ben are going to need it. The GPIRB is dead, the boat is slowly sinking, and the raft is damaged.

JP has the yellow GPIRB in his hand, shaking it, turning the switch on and off again and again, but still there is no light to indicate it's transmitting. *Did it ever send a signal?* he wonders. *When did it go dead?* Part of him doesn't want to tell the crew, but when he carries it down into the cabin, they know something is wrong by the look on his face. Then they see that the GPIRB's strobe is not working.

JP explains that the GPIRB and the life raft's canopy and the ballast bags are gone, adding that they need to stay with the boat as long as possible.

Rudy and Ben don't say a word. So much has happened in such a short period of time that they feel partly numb to the latest news. While JP was topside, they had been steadily bailing, throwing the water out the open companionway. Ben ingeniously cut the bottom out of a large water container to use as a scoop, and Rudy soon did the same. But despite their efforts, water is slowly rising inside the vessel.

Rudy pauses for a moment. His back, hurt from being thrown out of bed, seizes up, and he needs to rest. Two pumps are running, but both are continually clogging with debris and shutting down. Rudy realizes that they can't keep bailing indefinitely; soon the incoming water will overwhelm them. He wonders if they'll have any warning when the boat begins its descent to the bottom of the sea. As if answering his thought, a large wave slams the boat, knocking the men off their feet and into a bulkhead.

Rudy regains his footing and goes back to bailing, pausing only to snatch a floating apple, which he eats, thinking it may be some time before he sees food again.

JP is looking over the rest of his communications equipment. The satellite phone is soaked and out of commission, as is the single-side band radio. The primary VHF radio is also useless because its antenna, located on top of the mast, is lying in the water.

The boat does have two handheld VHF units that are still working. JP picks one up. "Mayday, Mayday, Mayday," he says. "This is the sailing vessel *Sean Seamour II*." He listens, not really expecting any answer. In good weather, JP estimates the hand-held VHF might broadcast thirty miles, but in the storm, he figures ten miles is its maximum range.

JP explains to Ben and Rudy that the handheld VHF radio is working, but its range is next to nothing. Still, periodically, one of the men will pick it up and call out a Mayday, hoping for a miracle.

It is now about four a.m., and the sailors are exhausted. Rudy, not understanding the full extent of the damage to the raft, approaches JP and says, "Maybe we should think about getting into the raft."

The captain shakes his head. "Let's wait longer, until we are sure the boat is sinking."

JP tries to help Rudy and Ben bail, but with broken ribs, he's unable to lift the scoop high enough to throw water out the companionway. He feels himself slowing down and wonders if he's going into shock. He is in pain, but even worse is the feeling that his thought process is beginning to cloud over. *Can this be hypothermia?* Whatever is happening scares him and stirs up waves of despair.

Too feeble and faint to bail, JP posts himself near one of the pumps to keep its intake free of debris. He tries to think through the evacuation into the life raft. Occasionally he pokes his head out the top of the companionway, letting his eyes adjust to mixed moonlight and cloud. Peering toward the bow, he decides, *When the bow is almost underwater, it's time to go.*

But not a moment before. He tells himself to stick to this plan no matter how strong the urge gets to leave the boat.

JP is hoping to avoid a life raft boarding in the dark, knowing that would pose double the danger. For the next hour, he monitors the waterline and notes that the water is slowly creeping upward. *Just hang on until daylight,* he says both to himself and to the *Sean Seamour II.*

Suddenly, at about five thirty, a large wave crashes directly on the boat, sending it careening down the face of the wave. The men are thrown to the starboard side, but amazingly, no one is injured.

The boat, however, doesn't fare as well. Green water blasts down the companionway, filling the vessel with an additional foot of seawater, bringing the level above the men's knees.

JP climbs the companionway, and from the cockpit he can see that the bow of his beloved boat is submerged. Holding his broken ribs, he turns and shouts back down toward Rudy and Ben, "Let's go! It's time to get out!"

∿

The first concern when boarding a life raft is the timing. You want to be in the life raft before the boat goes down, but not a minute before—a damaged boat is still safer than a life raft. The motion inside a boat is not as violent, and the boat is almost always drier, which is crucial to warding off hypothermia.

Keeping your body out of the water, or at least partially dry, is paramount, because water sucks away body heat twenty-five times as fast as air does.

When it comes to being rescued, the boat is also a better bet than a life raft because it's a bigger target for searchers in a plane or a passing ship. And the boat might have at least one radio working, allowing those in Mayday situations to broadcast as long as possible.

Life rafts may have some survival gear, but the boat will have far more. The boat will likely have extra food, water, a first-aid kit, clothes, PFDs, and flares. Once you are in the life raft, both supplies and options are fewer, and if the life raft gets flipped, the supplies might be swept away.

The old maritime saying "You've got to step up to the life raft" is a good one, reminding sailors not to board until they know the boat is sinking. But pithy sayings are difficult to follow in the actual chaos of a storm. On the flip side, if you wait too long to exit the vessel, there may not be enough time. Boats can and do sink suddenly. One minute a vessel can be slowly losing its battle to the sea, with water inching inside, and the next the bow plunges downward, the stern rears up, and the entire boat starts its slide to the bottom of the ocean.

All you can do is process the information as best as you can, then decide when the danger of staying on the boat exceeds that of being in a life raft. Factor in incredible fatigue or seasickness, and the right decision becomes even more difficult.

JP, Rudy, and Ben know they are going to get wet. The raft's canopy is gone, and the waves, at least seventy feet in height, will punish the raft like a little cork going down a raging river.

As the men prepare to climb out of the cabin, Rudy puts his wallet and passport in a plastic zip bag. "What the heck are you doing?" says Ben. "We're probably going to die, and we won't be needing those."

Ben has already come to terms with the notion that they won't be getting out of this jam. With the GPIRB not working and the old EPIRB not equipped with a hydrostatic release, he figures the Coast Guard never received their distress signal. And even if they did, Ben realizes that the only hope of rescue is by helicopter, and he thinks the winds are too strong for one to enter the storm. The only alternative is to give up, but he wants to go down fighting, wants to see the sky one last time. Rudy and JP, too, feel that their ultimate fate is death, but they're going to try to stay alive as long as they can.

All three men are calm as they prepare to exit the boat and enter the void. They tie themselves together with the tethers from their safety harnesses, hoping to avoid separation should they fall out of the raft. Rudy puts on the PFD he took off earlier, then stuffs his pockets with flares and a steak knife for cutting the raft free from the boat.

JP sees that his mates are ready. "Let's go," he says, slowly starting up the companionway steps, lugging a ditch bag with survival supplies behind him. In the bag is a handheld VHF radio, the satellite phone with extra batteries, food, water, flares, and other items necessary for survival at sea and assisting with rescue. Ben is next to climb the stairs. When it is Rudy's turn, he takes a last look around and grabs the dead GPIRB. He thinks, *We have nothing else, and even though it's dead, I might as well take it.*

When JP crawls into the cockpit, the tempest assaults him with shrieking wind and crashing seas. Thankfully, a gray dawn light helps them see, and JP notes with relief that the upside-down life raft is still secured to the vessel.

Ben and Rudy climb into the cockpit and get their first good look at the avalanching waves. Ben can't believe the size of the white-capped mountains of water surrounding him. One minute a wave towers above the boat; the next minute the vessel rises to the top, where Ben surveys foam-streaked waves in all directions. He has never seen such raw power, the absolute height of nature's fury, and he is awestruck.

The main line from the life raft to the boat is in a winch. JP stands on the elevated poop deck with his back against the steel arch and frees the line. By pulling on the line toward the port stern side of the boat, he manages to flip the raft right side up. He gasps for air, which causes him to wince in pain from the slight pressure on his ribs.

Suddenly, JP's eyes widen as he sees that the line that was

fastened to the drogue is severed a foot beyond where it was tied to a cleat on the boat. It is a clean break, and JP surmises it must have snapped like a rubber band during the first knockdown. There is no time to wonder if the vessel might have avoided the second disastrous capsizing had the drogue not snapped free—the bow of the boat is now completely submerged.

The raft is tight against the hull. With no canopy, and the boat riding low in the water, JP slides beneath the lifeline circling the boat and drops down into the raft. Ben follows, and then Rudy. Rudy realizes how exposed to the elements they will be. They sit in a flat area surrounded by an inflated tube; he likens it to being in a bathtub. He doesn't want to think about what will happen when they release from the boat.

Six inches of water splashes about inside the raft. The water temperature is seventy degrees Fahrenheit and does not feel cold to Rudy or Ben. They know they're lucky to be at the eastern edge of the Gulf Stream. If they were just a few miles off the western side instead, the May temperature of the ocean would be sixty degrees or lower.

The tether securing the raft to the boat needs to be cut, and Rudy does the job with the steak knife. Then he holds up the knife and looks at JP, who shouts, "Toss it! We don't want any sharp objects on the raft." Rudy quickly drops it into the ocean. The raft, however, does not float free of the sailboat. Waves batter it against the vessel, sending the men colliding against one another. Rudy, now on his knees, leans toward the sailboat and pushes the raft away as hard as he can. The raft bounces right back into the boat, sending Rudy backward into Ben. Twice more Rudy pushes against the boat, but the raft moves only three feet before slamming into the hull. The men frantically scan the outside of the raft. Rudy sees that there is a line leading back to the shredded canopy, which is caught on the *Sean Seamour II.*

Ben grabs Rudy's shoulder. Rudy turns to look at him and sighs with relief. Ben is holding up the rescue knife he purchased back in Jacksonville just a few days earlier. Since Rudy is sitting closest to the boat, he takes the knife from Ben and cuts the last remaining line. Rudy observes that the sailboat is nose-down in the water. A wave rolls under the raft, pushing it away, blocking the men's view of the sailboat. As the wave passes, the men stare at where the boat should be. It is gone. The ocean has swallowed the *Sean Seamour II* into its dark and unforgiving depths.

THE CUTTER *TAMPA*
AND THE C-130

The cutter *Tampa* is headed into the teeth of the storm, plowing toward the coordinates from EPIRB hits transmitted by the *Flying Colours* and the *Sean Seamour II.* Waves batter the cutter, and the ninety-seven men and women aboard are bracing themselves, struggling to maintain their positions. At least a third of the crew are seasick, and all are tired from trying to maintain their balance to offset the constant motion of the ship.

The 270-foot-long cutter left the coast of New Jersey a few hours earlier but is at least twenty-four hours away from the distress scene. The maximum speed of the cutter is twenty knots, but because the vessel is steaming into waves of twenty feet, the fastest headway it can make is between fourteen and sixteen knots. Executive Officer Charles Fosse has never been in waves this large and menacing. Already some Coasties have cuts and bruises from being knocked off their feet when the seas rolled the vessel thirty degrees. During one particularly vicious hit from a wave, so much water avalanched onto the deck that it entered the ventilation system; crew members felt like it was raining inside the cutter.

Sending a cutter on a rescue mission in a storm of this magnitude has its own set of risks. Take the case of the cutters *Bedloe* and *Jackson*, both 125 feet long and weighing 220 tons. During a massive hurricane in September 1944, later named the Great Atlantic Hurricane, the two cutters were dispatched to aid a Liberty ship in distress just off the coast of North Carolina. Waves were topping out at eighty feet, and neither of the cutters could withstand the liquid walls of water tossing them about like so much flotsam. A few miles off Oregon Inlet, both cutters suffered knockdowns and filled with so much water that they started to sink.

William Ruhl, aboard the *Jackson*, was in the galley when the ship began a roll and kept going over. Green seawater poured through a broken hatch, and Ruhl scrambled up the passageway onto the deck, forgetting his life jacket in the dash to escape being trapped. "The waves were like mountains rolling over the ship," he later recalled. The ship was on its side, and Ruhl was swimming in the ocean. Luckily, a raft, torn from the deck of the ship, was bobbing in the water nearby, and Ruhl heaved himself inside. Six other Coasties found their way into the tiny raft, but others were not so lucky.

In the raft, the survivors assumed that help would be coming from the *Bedloe* soon, not knowing that their sister ship had sunk as well. The men made it through the night, but when it became apparent that help was not imminent, two of them tried to swim ashore. They swam for three hours with little progress and turned back when they saw a shark circling.

For the next fifty hours, those six men bailed, prayed, and hung on as best they could. Coast Guard Kingfisher planes with pontoons for landing in water eventually spotted the raft and landed the aircraft in the swells. The aircrew shed their clothes, jumped into the water, and hoisted the survivors onto the wings of the plane, where they administered first aid while awaiting rescue boats from Oregon Inlet.

Two other rafts were located, and survivors explained that several men had died during the second night from exposure and exhaustion. William McCreedy was on board a rescue boat and recalled that when he approached one of the rafts, a man inside jumped overboard and became tangled in a trailing line. McCreedy dove into the water, cut the man free, and with the aid of crewmates, hoisted him into the boat. As they were heading back to shore with other survivors, the man who had jumped overboard touched McCreedy's face and said, "We made it." Those were his last words—a moment later, he died.

A total of forty-eight Coasties from the *Jackson* and the *Bedloe* perished during that ill-fated mission. The Liberty ship stayed afloat with no casualties and was later towed to shore.

Now, in the storm that has sunk the *Sean Seamour II,* the Coasties aboard the *Tampa* are putting themselves in grave peril.

~

Besides the *Tampa*, the other resource being sent into the storm is the C-130 Hercules, a long-range fixed-wing aircraft, a real workhorse for the Coast Guard. This four-engine turboprop plane was originally designed as a troop, medical evacuation, and cargo transport plane. It has been in continuous production for more than fifty years, used primarily by the U.S. Air Force, the Marine Corps, and the Coast Guard. The Coast Guard has modified the aircraft for search and rescue as well as reconnaissance and patrol. Compared with the Coast Guard helicopters that work with the C-130 on rescue missions, the plane looks enormous. It has a length of 97 feet, a wingspan of 132 feet, and an empty weight of 76,000 pounds.

The Coast Guard uses a crew of seven for C-130 rescue missions. In the flight deck, the pilot sits in the left seat, the copilot in the right, and directly behind them the flight engineer. Next are two seats for the navigator and the radio operator. Three steps down from the flight deck is the cavernous cargo compartment, filled with life rafts, radios, survival suits, flares, and dewatering pumps. Two more Coasties sit in this area—the drop master and a basic air crew member. They can open the ramp door in the rear of the aircraft and push out pieces of survival equipment to people in distress below. Usually, this equipment is deployed by parachute unless the wind is extreme. If they need to drop flares or a data buoy marker that measures drift rates, they can open paratroop doors on either the left or right of the cargo compartment. When the drop master and the basic air crewman are not deploying equipment, they have access to two side windows, from which they can assist the other crew members scanning the ocean for survivors.

The C-130 flying toward the *Sean Seamour II* and *Flying Colours* is under the command of Paul Beavis, flight commander. He has a crew of six: Copilot Ed Ahlstrand, Flight Engineer Stacy Sorenson, Navigator Marcus Jones, Radioman Jesse Bennett, Drop Master Casey Green, and Air Crewman Ryan Cantu.

The farther out to sea they fly, the more turbulent the ride. Heavy rain begins to fall when they are one hundred miles out, and the crew know the search won't be easy. When they are about fifty miles from the closest EPIRB hit, they begin descending, not stopping until they are below cloud cover at just four hundred feet above the ocean. The radioman begins making broadcasts, trying to hail one of the vessels in distress, but no one answers.

Dawn has provided a bit of light, but the rain makes

visibility poor. The turbulence is severe, causing the plane to lurch. Jones braces himself to help stabilize his vision. He has been in the Coast Guard seven years and logged more than three thousand hours aboard C-130s, and he's never been in weather like this.

Through the rain-swept windshield, Commander Beavis gets his first look at the waves, and they are beyond anything he has encountered. He watches a wave break into a chaotic brew of crashing foam, and it appears that the white water stretches longer than a city block. They are now on scene, and the aircraft is flying in racetrack-pattern loops, each extending farther from the center. It is the turns that put Beavis on edge. They have to roll the plane to a thirty-degree angle on each turn. With wind blasts of eighty knots and their low proximity to the water, the commander has plenty to worry about. He is using every bit of concentration to keep the four-hundred-foot altitude steady and not bank too steeply. There's a fine line between keeping the plane low enough to have any hope at spotting a boat or raft, yet protecting it from the enormous waves, which could clip the wing closest to the water while they're banking.

Beavis knows that the lives of his crew are in his hands, as well as the life of anyone on a boat below. He also knows that if any of the sailors are in the water, it will be nearly impossible to spot them. He's not even sure his crew can pick a life raft out of the cauldron below.

12

TUMBLING IN CHAOS

JP's beloved boat is gone, and with it his outside link to the world. He stares at the empty spot in the ocean where the boat was just a couple of seconds earlier. He tries to think ahead and searches for the bright yellow grab bag he had filled with supplies. It, too, is gone. He remembers dropping it in the cockpit and shouting for one of the others to carry it into the raft while he released the tether from the winch. But with the shrieking wind and blinding spray, neither Rudy nor Ben heard JP or saw the bag. *It sank with the boat,* he thinks. It was much too heavy to float. Of all the supplies in the bag, the men most need water and flares. They have no other source of water, and JP is not sure if Rudy stuffed a few flares in his foul-weather gear at the last moment. Whatever survival supplies might have come prepackaged with the raft have been swept away, probably when it was impaled by the mast and dragged next to the boat.

JP's brain and body seem to be crashing at the same time. He watches Rudy and Ben try to cover themselves with a small piece of canopy, though it is repeatedly blown away. In a weak voice, JP rasps, "It's useless." The lack of a canopy not only means the raft will stay full of water no matter how much they bail; it also reduces their odds of being spotted by a plane. The canopy is a bright fluorescent orange, but the raft itself is black and blends in with the dark ocean. Making matters worse is that without the ballast bags hanging below, the little vessel is less stable and more susceptible to flipping. It slides wildly with the waves, and whenever it reaches a crest, the men feel as if they are at the edge of a cliff. They are afraid they will be thrown from the raft, so they use the clips at the end of their safety harness tethers to fasten themselves to a lifeline inside the raft.

Ben stares at the oncoming walls of water and is struck by the utter despair he feels in his surroundings: gray skies, gray waves, and white streaks of foam where the tops of the giant combers meet the sky. The water is seething in every direction. The only thing between the men and the lethal seas is the three fabric tubes encircling the floor of the raft.

None of the three men talk. All have arrived at the same conclusion: *No one is coming for us.* Rudy thinks, *Even if we manage to stay in the raft, we aren't going to live long.* He glances at JP and notices the captain's skin color is a sickly gray, as if his blood isn't circulating properly. Rudy wonders if JP is in shock from his injury and if he has entered the early stages of hypothermia. He worries that his friend isn't going to make it another hour.

While the seventy-degree water temperature might seem relatively warm, in time it will kill anyone who stays submerged or partially submerged. The first victim would be JP, because he is short and slim. When cold starts to suck away the body's heat, larger, heavier people fare much better than small, thin people. JP is also completely exhausted, which won't help in his battle to generate body heat. The first body parts to be affected are the fingers and toes, where there is little fat to insulate the blood from the heat-sapping water. These extremities will become numb and stiff, and JP will lose dexterity. In essence, the body yields these extremities to the cold, reducing blood flow to the area in an effort to keep the core— particularly the heart—warm. Next to go will be the arms and legs, making it hard to swim. If JP is swept from the raft at an advanced stage of hypothermia, he won't be able to stroke back. He will die from drowning long before the loss of body heat causes his heart to give out. Many hypothermic victims lose consciousness and die when they can no longer keep their heads out of the water. This usually happens when the body's core temperature drops to eighty-seven degrees.

Most people think they must keep moving to keep the blood circulating and generate body heat, but that just expends precious energy. A person in cold water should conserve energy by minimizing movement. Loss of body heat can be slowed by holding your knees to your chest to help keep the upper torso warm. And two people can help fight off hypothermia by huddling together, chest to chest.

JP is helped by the fact that he is fully clothed in foul-weather gear, which traps a bit of body heat. But most of the body's warmth escapes from the head, and he has no hat on. If the raft's canopy were up, that would reduce the loss of heat from windchill, but JP is sitting and shivering in a half foot of water, completely exposed to the hurricane-force winds. The involuntary shivering is his body's way of trying to produce a little warmth in its fight against the cold.

Adding to the effects of hypothermia will be dehydration; it, too, causes the blood to thicken with decreased volume. The symptoms of dehydration include a reduction in mental abilities, slurred speech, and overall inefficiency—the same problems caused by hypothermia. A person needs two quarts of water a day to maintain health, and soon all three men will be parched. They will have to fight the urge to sip seawater, which only makes the problems worse—the salt dehydrates the body, causing hallucinations. JP's slow-circulating blood is restricting the flow of oxygen to his brain, and that, along with shock, is the cause of his mental sluggishness. If the hypothermia advances, the blood will thicken further, making clear thought all but impossible. Help will have to come soon, or the hypothermia will continue its silent march toward his brain and vital organs.

For now, JP drifts in and out of consciousness. He has resigned himself to death. He feels the same sad helplessness that he did at the burn hospital, knowing there is nothing more he can do for himself or his crew. The storm was just too much for him and his *Sean Seamour II*. He fights the urge to drift off for good. It's not time yet.

The raft, pushed by the wind and waves, is traveling at an incredible nine knots—it is already miles from the site where the EPIRB indicated the emergency. The sounds of the ocean rise and fall with the waves. When the sailors are in the trough, the crashing seas are muffled slightly. As the raft rides toward the crest, however, the roaring increases until they teeter on the top and are exposed to the full fury of the howling wind.

After about twenty minutes in the raft, disaster strikes. An enormous wave slides under the raft, lifting it higher and higher. As the vessel nears the crest, the steep wave can no longer support itself and comes crashing down directly on the raft. It slams into the men with the impact of a train.

The raft is flipped like a pancake, and the men go flying and tumbling. In the trough, Rudy and Ben, still tethered to the raft, realize they are under the overturned vessel, and they quickly unclip and kick to the surface. Salt stings their eyes as they search for JP. Rudy ducks beneath the raft to find JP struggling with his tether. Rudy, not yet feeling any real effects of hypothermia, is able to unclip JP and bring him out from under the raft. Another wave towers over the men, ready to pounce and pile-drive them under and finish them off. Thankfully, this second wave is not as steep as the first, and it doesn't break but instead slides under the three sailors. In the second trough, Rudy hears JP mumbling, and he leans closer. "Ben, Ben, where's Ben?" says JP.

"He's on the other side of the raft!" shouts Rudy. "He's okay!" Rudy is thankful JP is thinking and able to hold his head up. He's not sure he could grip the outside of the raft and support JP's head at the same time.

Ben inches his way around the raft, and together they try to pull the raft right side up. It doesn't budge. Another wave bears down on them. They are carried out of the trough up into the shrieking wind before the wave continues on. Ben notices that most waves are not breaking but just have small curls of white water at the top, and for that he is thankful. If wave after wave were breaking, they would be either free-falling or driven deep underwater every forty to fifty seconds. None of them would be alive within an hour's time.

They try pushing the raft over but again have no luck. Ben and Rudy talk in the trough of the waves and decide that if they can all get downwind, perhaps they can work with the blasting gusts to flip the raft back into its proper position. Using the lifeline that encircles the raft, they kick to the downwind side, helping JP as best they can. They let another wave slip under them, and when they're near the top, where the wind is strongest, Rudy and Ben pull down on the raft, trying to get the opposite end off the water so the wind can work its way underneath and help finish the job.

The far side of the raft rides up a little bit, as they hoped, but soon they are back down in the trough, where they are somewhat sheltered from the wind. Again and again they try the technique, but the exhausted men have no luck. They hang on for a few minutes, until another steep wave breaks on them, as if trying to pound them into submission. They come up coughing and gagging but still have hold of the raft.

Hypothermia will advance more quickly now that every part of their bodies is submerged except their heads. They are expending valuable energy just hanging on to the raft's life-line, craning their necks so they don't breathe in foam or get a mouthful of water. If they stay like this, they won't have to worry about hypothermia—the storm will finish them off by drowning them.

CONVULSIONS

Water pours off Rudy's gray beard. The sixty-two-year-old is being worn down by the effort to hold on to the overturned life raft. But he is also pissed off. It seems he and his mates can't get a break. First the storm behaved differently than forecast; next the GPIRB didn't work properly; and then the life raft got pinned by the mast. And now, a couple of hours after the men abandoned ship, the storm seems to have singled them out for punishment by not allowing them to flip the raft right side up. His anger is simmering, and soon it produces adrenaline and strength. Rudy lets go of the lifeline and tries to flip the raft by brute force. He gets his arms around the top of the inflated tubes, and with a sudden kick from his legs along with a push-up motion from his arms, he hoists the upper half of his body onto the overturned raft. He heaves his legs up and collapses facedown on top of the raft. It's a remarkable display of strength, considering he is in waterlogged clothing and foul-weather gear.

Once Rudy catches his breath, he assists Ben in crawling on top. Then the men each grab one of JP's arms and haul him up. The overturned raft looks like a trampoline, and the three men have to lie prone on it so they don't slip off. They do their best to hide their heads from the wind-driven rain that stings their exposed skin, as if someone has taken a handful of gravel and thrown it point-blank into their faces. Ben and Rudy position themselves on either side of JP so he doesn't fall out. JP is shaking from the cold, and Ben worries that he won't last another hour. Waves are crashing around them, though fortunately none make a direct hit on the raft. Ben inches closer to JP so that he is almost on top of him, trying to share his body heat and shield JP from the wind. A bit of canopy is swaying in the waterlogged raft, and Ben tries to cover JP with it, but there isn't enough of the fabric to do any good.

JP's mind is lucid one moment and foggy the next. He's in the fetal position, his arms and legs tucked in tight, his lips blue. The wind knifes right through his slender frame, and he sadly remembers the survival suits stowed on the boat. They were impossible to access because the broken mast had landed directly on the deck locker where the suits were stowed. The mast was too heavy for the men to lift high enough to open the locker top.

JP knows he is close to the end. He can feel himself con-
vulsing, and the pain from his broken ribs is excruciating. He
thinks of his wife, Mayke, in France and wants to tell her that
he loves her, that he's sorry for taking this voyage, that he has
done his best.

He tries to talk to Rudy. "Tell Mayke . . ."

Rudy can't understand the rest, but he's sure JP knows he
is dying and wants Rudy to pass on a message of love to his
wife. Rudy doesn't bother to ask JP to repeat himself. *It's not
going to matter,* Rudy thinks. *None of us will be alive to tell anybody
anything.*

Rudy looks at JP and tries to hold the captain's head in his
arms. JP's entire body convulses twice, then doesn't move at
all. *Is he dead?* wonders Rudy.

Then, pow! A mammoth wave avalanches onto the raft,
sending the men into the sea and the raft arching into the air.
The churning water engulfs them as though they have gone
over a waterfall and are in the vortex below.

Ben and Rudy come up choking, gasping for air. They can't
see JP anywhere. The raft is nearby, and Ben grabs hold of it.
Rudy does the same. The raft is now right side up, but they
don't even notice—they're craning their necks, trying to spot
JP. Rudy kicks to gain an inch or two of height above the
foam, and in the process, he sees JP drifting at least twenty feet
away. The Canadian swims to JP, clutches the hood of his
friend's foul-weather gear, and drags him back to the raft.

Ben helps Rudy keep a firm grip on JP, and all three men

catch their breath. If another wave breaks on the raft, they will lose their hold on it, and the raft will be swept away. Now they notice that the raft is right side up, and this gives them hope. Rudy can see the GPIRB tethered to the middle of the raft, and he thinks, *No wonder the raft was impossible to turn over; the GPIRB was hanging down like an anchor when the raft first flipped.*

JP seems conscious but is staring off into the distance. Rudy shouts, "Hang on! We'll get you back in the raft." JP neither looks at him nor responds. In actuality, JP does hear snatches of Rudy's voice, but it seems miles away. His mind is in a sort of limbo, and he can't feel the pain anymore.

Once again Rudy pulls himself into the raft and, with Ben's help, hoists JP up. Then Ben climbs in, and all three men collapse in a heap, each lost in his own thoughts.

JP feels like he is leaving for somewhere else. His eyes are open, and he looks at the charging combers with wonder. When waves collide, pillars of water shoot high above the seventy-foot mountains, filling the air like geysers. And when they're down in the canyons, JP thinks the sheer walls around him are the most spectacular thing he has ever seen. He feels at peace, ready to die.

Rudy is also thinking about death. He figures he will be dead soon, so he tries to ease his tension by focusing on the waves. In a sense, Rudy is detaching from the situation and looking at it like an observer. He attempts to measure the waves in increments of ten feet. Starting at the bottom of a trough, he slowly looks up. *Okay, here is the first ten feet, here is the next ten feet.* He continues counting off the sections of the gray liquid wall rising closest to him. When he reaches eighty feet, he is so surprised that he repeats the process, with the same result. *Even if I'm off by ten feet, these waves have got to be at least seventy feet. This is unbelievable, absolutely incredible.* He is fully engaged in the process of observing, almost as if he's at a movie theater, looking at astonishing images flickering on the screen. The Gulf Stream is putting on the ultimate show, and Rudy knows he is witnessing something only a handful of people on earth have ever seen.

Rudy wonders how long the thin fabric of the raft can hold out against the beating. He figures a few more hours, which is probably longer than they can hang on, considering it has already flipped twice. Losing the ballast bags, reasons Rudy, makes the raft little better than a child's inflatable pool. His mind starts to drift to what will happen after he's gone, what his children will do with his affairs and what their future lives will be like.

Ben is just as calm as the others and tries to think ahead a few hours. *Even if we outlast the storm—which could go on for days—we have no drinking water.* He is aware that hypothermia will likely kill them long before dehydration, but he doesn't feel cold. When he was younger, doing his dinghy sailing off the English coast, the temperatures were always cold, so this current exposure doesn't have an impact on him. Still, he knows that their only chance is if the GPIRB transmitted correctly before it went dead.

In a trough, Ben asks Rudy, a trained pilot, "Do you think a helicopter could fly in these conditions?"

Rudy looks out at the crest of the waves, noting how the wind rips spray off their tops, hurling it sideways through the air. "Probably not."

"Didn't think so," says Ben. He wonders if there is anything he can do to help their situation. Bailing would be futile. The flares are useless unless someone is searching for them. But he keeps wondering if he has missed any opportunity to improve their lot, if only to make JP a little more comfortable.

The three men are like soldiers on a battlefield, vastly outnumbered and outgunned, cut off from all help. They know they will be overrun, know they are going to die, but still they defend their little piece of turf, the raft.

PART III

NEED MAX GAS

A ringing telephone wakes up Nevada Smith and his wife at five thirty a.m. at their home in Camden, North Carolina, about four miles from Air Station Elizabeth City. Nevada, a seasoned Coast Guard helicopter pilot, and his Colombian-born wife, Julieta, are used to such early-morning calls. Julieta answers the phone, then tosses it to Nevada, saying in a soft accent, "It's those Coast Guard guys again."

On the other end of the line is the operation duty officer (ODO) at Air Station Elizabeth City. "We're having a busy morning. We got some aircraft out right now, and we need another H60 (helicopter) crew. We have a couple EPIRBs going off about 220 nautical miles to the southeast. The Herc [C-130] is on its way right now. When can you get here?"

Nevada says, "I'll be there in thirty minutes. I'll need max gas." (Translation: Add a 120-gallon fuel tank and fill all four tanks—three external and one internal—to maximum capacity, about 6,300 pounds of gas.) A large man at six feet four and 250 pounds, he is now wide awake. "I'm on my way."

Running a hand through his thinning blond hair, he throws on some clothes, then hops in his 1968 Jeep, heading for the air station. He's looking forward to this case because he knows a C-130 will soon be in the vicinity of the distress calls, and that means he'll probably be able to focus on the rescue rather than the searching.

Born at the U.S. Naval Air Station in Pensacola, Florida, in 1967, Nevada is the son of a Navy E-2 Hawkeye pilot. It's not surprising that Nevada wanted to fly from the time he was a little boy, and on every Christmas and birthday, he would ask that his presents include model airplanes. "Over the holidays, I was knocking out model airplanes," recalls Nevada, "like Henry Ford made Model Ts. I had an assembly line going of World War Two bombers and fighters." More than thirty airplanes hung from the ceiling of his bedroom, and he started calling it "the Nevada Smithsonian Air Museum." He always got a hoot out of being born in the cradle of naval aviation—Pensacola, Florida, where all U.S. Navy, Coast Guard, and Marine Corps pilots start their training. Even his initials are N.A.S., which stands for not only *Nevada Allen Smith* but also *Naval Air Station*.

During his early teen years, Nevada, who was bigger and

taller than most of his peers, was encouraged by friends and coaches to play football and basketball. He wasn't interested. Rather than choosing Joe Montana and Julius Erving as his heroes, Nevada idolized pilots: Billy Mitchell, Pappy Boyington, Paul Tibbets, the Wright brothers, Chuck Yeager, and his father and all his dad's ex-Navy flying buddies. He wanted to be like those guys.

Upon graduating from high school, Nevada went to college at Southern Illinois University at Edwardsville and joined the U.S. Air Force ROTC program. His dream of the Air Force, however, was short-lived: He was half an inch too tall to properly fit in the cockpit of a fighter jet. It was disappointing but not devastating, because Nevada, then nineteen, could still fly for the seagoing services—the Navy, the Marine Corps, or the Coast Guard. He transferred to Iowa State and spent another year in Navy ROTC. The out-of-state tuition was quite high, and his dad offered him an alternative: if Nevada transferred to college in Carbondale, Illinois, he could use the savings to pay for flight lessons.

After securing his pilot's license, Nevada spent much of his free time reading about pilots and aircraft. While looking through an aviation magazine, he read an article about the new HH-60J Jayhawk helicopters that the Coast Guard would soon add to its inventory. His eyes lingered on a picture of an H-60 medium-range helicopter used by the Coast Guard for search and rescue. It was love at first sight.

Prior to his graduation from college, he applied to the Coast

Guard's officer candidate school (OCS) but was rejected. At first he was devastated. Then he thought, *That's not going to stop me. I'll enlist!* He was living in the small town of Roscoe, Illinois, a few miles south of the Wisconsin border, about two hours from Chicago. He told his mother he was driving to the Coast Guard's recruiting office in Chicago. His mother reminded him not to sign anything before talking to his father.

Nevada went to Chicago and signed every form the recruiter put in front of him. He took the Armed Services Vocational Aptitude Battery Test in a run-down brick building in Rockford, Illinois. After the test, he got in his car and heard that the bombing of Baghdad had started. He was off to boot camp in Cape May, New Jersey, just a few weeks later—February 1991, during the Gulf War.

Upon graduation from boot camp, Nevada was turned down a second time for OCS. Instead, he did a tour on a buoy tender on the Mississippi River. After that assignment, he once again tried to gain entry into OCS, and this time he was accepted. His good fortune continued when the Coast Guard sent him to the extremely demanding Navy flight school in Pensacola, Florida. When he earned his wings of gold in 1995, his father pinned the same wings on his son that he had earned twenty-six years earlier. Over the next few years, Nevada flew on dozens of SAR missions, including rescuing victims of Hurricane Katrina. In 2005, he auditioned for the movie *The Guardian* and landed the role of Lieutenant Ken Krauss. It was an exciting time for the young pilot: he spent two weeks filming in Shreveport, Louisiana, followed by two days in Elizabeth City and one in Hollywood.

Now, arriving at Air Station Elizabeth City, Nevada is thinking that today's SAR mission will be relatively routine. Rain is falling, with wind gusts up to thirty knots—the usual nasty weather he flies in. He parks his Jeep, runs into the Operations Center, and dons his flight suit. The watch captain on duty informs him that he will be the aircraft commander, and his copilot will be Aaron Nelson.

Normally, in the lower forty-eight states, the commander takes the right seat to monitor the hoist, but Nevada knows Aaron is an amazing pilot and decides he will be in the right seat and Nevada in the left. Although Aaron has been in the Coast Guard only three years, he has more flying experience than Nevada does. The thirty-five-year-old pilot grew up in North Dakota, but unlike Nevada, he didn't make flying a career goal until his junior year of high school. His guidance counselor noticed he wasn't applying himself to his studies, yet he still was a B student. The counselor asked what he wanted to do with his life. Aaron hadn't given it much thought, but because his brother was in the Air Force, he said, "I'd like to fly planes." The counselor said he might be able to help, and he walked Aaron through the steps necessary to get into the Air Force Academy. "You need to get in shape," said the counselor, "and have a near-perfect GPA. Start taking tougher courses, like physics."

This challenge was exactly what Aaron needed, and with a

new sense of purpose, he began to exercise daily and earn straight As. A friend offered further motivation when he started taking flying lessons and invited Aaron to come along. Aaron sat in the backseat and watched his friend and the instructor go through the preflight checklist. When the plane zipped down the runway and was airborne, Aaron knew he wanted to pilot one. He soon found a part-time job and used the income for his own flight lessons, getting his pilot's license about the time he graduated from high school. His goal to go to the Air Force Academy was derailed when he was rejected, apparently because of his B average prior to his junior year.

Aaron's father pointed out another path, saying that the Army warrant officer pilots fly every day.

Within a week, Aaron was talking to Army recruiters about the warrant officer flight training program. Since Aaron didn't have a college degree, the recruiters set the bar high, telling him, "You not only have to pass all the tests—you have to score above average."

Aaron did well on the tests, and a few months later, he went through basic training and then on to U.S. Army flight school at the age of nineteen. Upon graduation, he was stationed in Germany, then Hawaii, flying primarily Black Hawk helicopters. After eight years, Aaron left the active-duty Army and flew for two commercial airlines while continuing to fly Black Hawk helicopters part-time in the Hawaii Army National Guard. In 2004, now married with children, Aaron decided to take a flying position with the Coast Guard and was assigned to Elizabeth City. He was often teamed with Nevada Smith, and the two men worked well together. On the morning of May 7, 2007, they were headed out for yet another mission.

~

While the two pilots are being briefed in the Operations Center, they are joined by Flight Mechanic Scott Higgins and Aviation Survival Technician (rescue swimmer) Drew Dazzo. Nevada is glad to see both men; he now has a very experienced crew.

Nevada conducts a prebrief with his team, explaining that two sailboats have activated their EPIRBs about 220 nautical miles out to sea off North Carolina. There is little other information to go on, because the C-130 has yet to make radio contact with those in distress. Reports coming back from the C-130 describe how the wind gusts are getting higher and higher as the plane approaches the emergency site. This mission that Nevada thought would be routine is beginning to look quite challenging. He and his crew assume the offshore seas are extreme for two boats to have activated their EPIRBs, but none of the men imagine they are going into a storm with winds over hurricane force.

"Make sure we have the external fuel tank on," says Nevada to Scott, "and max fuel." Both men know the HH-60 Jayhawk might need every drop of fuel going so far offshore to multiple EPIRBs with little concrete information. Scott, like Nevada, is thankful that each member of the crew has been around long enough to have participated in all sorts of SARs and flown into just about every kind of weather.

Scott feels at somewhat of a disadvantage because they have so little information to go on. Normally, he tries to glean every fact from the prebriefing that will help him, such as the heading of the vessel in distress, its speed, and the condition of survivors. He especially wants to know whether the people in distress are ambulatory. Whether or not they can move on their own can influence his decision to use a basket or a litter, which is larger and more difficult to maneuver. He wants to be prepared so that when he arrives on scene, he will have gone over the rescue plans with Drew. On this case, they have no idea what to expect and little information about the sea conditions so far offshore.

When he got the call at home, Scott thought it was just another false alarm. Outside his bedroom window, only a light breeze was blowing. In his twelve years with the Coast Guard, 80 percent of the SAR cases he flew on turned out to be false alarms or hoaxes.

The four crew members gather outside on the tarmac at their helicopter. Nevada yells to Scott, "I'll be in the left seat, running things. Lieutenant Nelson will be in the right seat, so he'll be working with you on the hoists. He's a better pilot than I am, anyway."

Scott nods, and then each man gives the helicopter a once-over to make sure everything is in order and nothing is

Jean Pierre (JP) de Lutz is fifty-seven years old and the owner of the *Sean Seamour II*.
[Courtesy Jean Pierre de Lutz]

Rudy Snel, from Ottawa, Canada, has recently retired from a career of teaching in public schools and now has time to follow his dream of making a long sailing voyage.
[Courtesy Rudy Snel]

Ben Tye at the wheel. Ben is from the United Kingdom. [Courtesy Ben Tye]

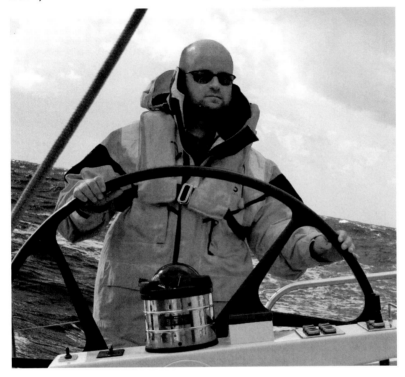

A forty-four-foot sailboat, the *Sean Seamour II* is JP's pride and joy.
[Courtesy Jean Pierre de Lutz]

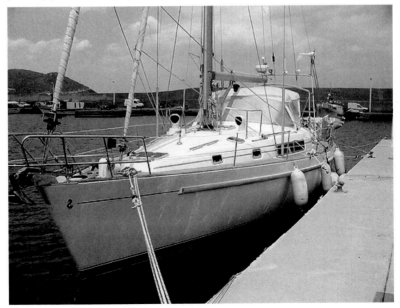

The men were planning to sail northeast, pass the northern side of
Bermuda, and then continue on to France. The Gulf Stream flows not far
offshore in a northeastward direction.

The location of the *Sean Seamour II* when the storm hit.

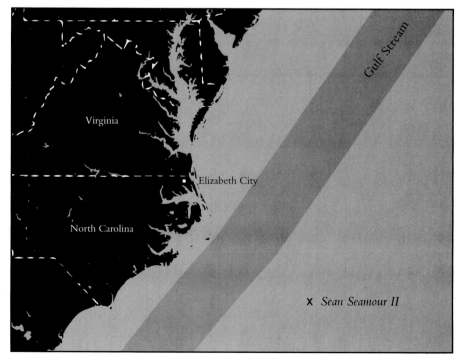

The Coast Guard rescue team from left to right: Drew Dazzo, Scott Higgins, Nevada Smith, and Aaron Nelson. [Courtesy U.S. Coast Guard]

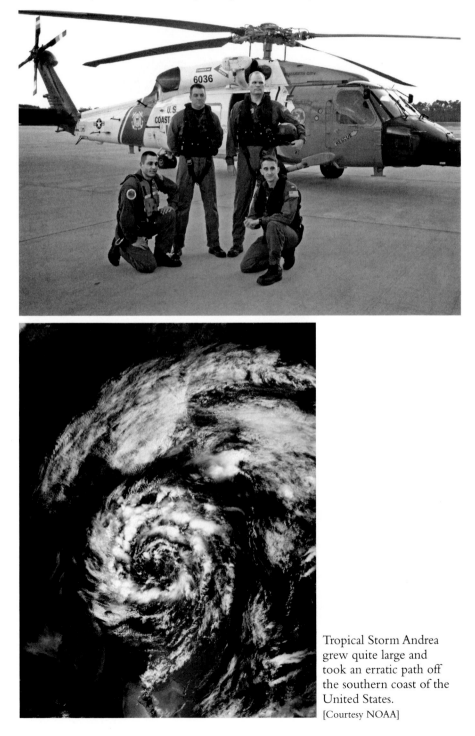

Tropical Storm Andrea grew quite large and took an erratic path off the southern coast of the United States. [Courtesy NOAA]

A view of breaking seas from the deck of the Coast Guard cutter *Tampa* during the storm. [Courtesy U.S. Coast Guard]

This photo of the life raft that JP, Ben, and Rudy were in was taken by a Coast Guard aircraft crewman. The eighty-foot wave makes the life raft look tiny! [Courtesy Nevada Smith]

Scott Higgins is leaning out of the helicopter to help guide the cable. In this picture, all that can be seen is the lower half of his body sprawled on the floor of the helicopter cabin.
[Courtesy Nevada Smith]

Scott is lifting Rudy out of the basket while JP tries to help.
[Courtesy Nevada Smith]

Rudy (with the beard) and JP are safely inside the helicopter.
[Courtesy Nevada Smith]

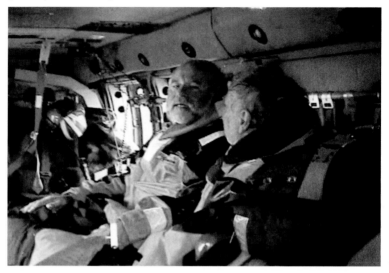

Once the helicopter lands, the injured and hypothermic men are whisked away to a hospital. Nevada Smith is looking on as he stands by the front of the helicopter. [Courtesy U.S. Coast Guard]

Rudy and JP a couple of months after the rescue. Each saved the other man's life.
[Courtesy Rudy Snel]

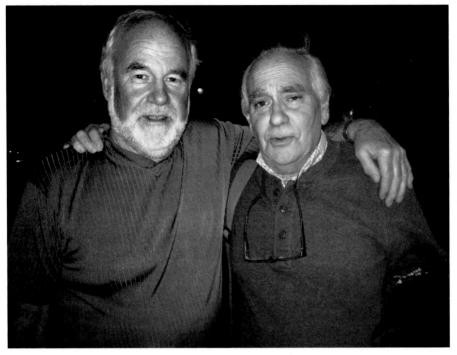

Rudy looks on as Drew holds the Canadian Star of Courage he was awarded.
[Courtesy Rudy Snel]

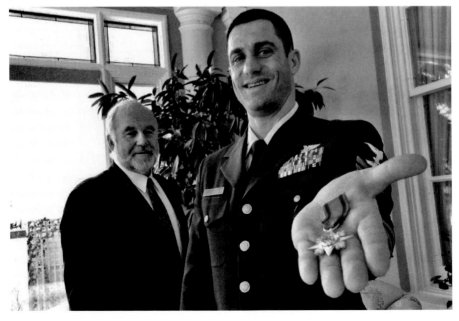

missing. Scott and Drew check inside the cabin for the rescue equipment, along with the medical supplies. Drew is the flight's emergency medical technician, and it will be his job to stabilize and assist any injured survivors.

The Jayhawk is a large aircraft, at seventeen feet in height and sixty-five feet in length, and its four main rotors have a diameter of fifty-four feet. It can fly at speeds of up to 170 knots, although the helicopter cruises best at 140 knots. The cockpit contains what seems, to the non-aviation observer, an almost overwhelming number of instruments and switches. The pilots monitor their instruments to be sure the helicopter's systems are performing properly. They also scan the horizon for other aircraft, boats, and the sea conditions. Fortunately, the cockpit has windows in the front, at foot level, on the sides, and even above.

A video camera mounted on the underbelly of the aircraft can project a picture on a monitor in front of the pilots. This allows them to see a small partial area beneath them. But the camera can't paint the image that the hoist operator is able to give the pilots of what is happening in the water below, particularly in regard to the cable and the rescue swimmer. The cable is two hundred feet long and surprisingly thin, about the size of a pinkie finger. It is composed of dozens of woven steel strands, which give it the strength to hoist up to eleven thousand pounds of weight. As tough as the cable is, the strands can fray if it rubs up against any part of the helicopter. If this happens, the real danger is not that the cable will break but that it will start to unravel and get stuck in the spool. This situation means that the rescue swimmer and a survivor can get stuck halfway between the helicopter and the water, or left in the water with no way to extract them.

Depending on weather conditions and wind direction, the Jayhawk's fuel can fly a crew of four about three hundred miles out to sea, conduct a rescue lasting forty-five minutes, and have enough gas left in the tanks to return to land. Nevada wants max fuel because he doesn't know how long it will take to locate the vessel or people in the water. Nor does he know the wave heights that will play a role in how long Drew might have to be in the ocean.

One of the primary instruments Nevada and Aaron will monitor at the rescue site is the radar altimeter, which tells them the helicopter's height from the ocean. The pilots need to keep the aircraft low enough that Scott can manage the cable and get Drew as close as possible to the survivors, but high enough that it doesn't get hit by a wave. If enough water hits the engines, they will flame out, and the helicopter will drop like a stone. When it hits the sea, it doesn't stay upright but, rather, "turtles." The large, heavy rotors pull the body of the aircraft to one side or the other, and the helicopter quickly goes upside down. That is why all four crew members have completed a grueling water course with a simulator, meant to train them to exit an aircraft in the water. The simulator is called "the Dunker," and the crew is strapped into their seats wearing blacked-out goggles and full flight suits. The Dunker is dropped into a swimming pool and rolled upside down, and the crew has to escape. They learn to orient themselves, using handholds to feel their way out. If necessary they can grab a small amount of air from a tiny oxygen tank called a helicopter emergency egress device (HEED). More than one airman has had recurring nightmares from this most harrowing form of training. Yet if a real crash occurs, this is exactly the hellish situation they will be in, only a lot more violent.

The threat of such a scenario is very real and has happened more than once in the last ten years. One of the more publicized incidents was the December 2004 crash of a Jayhawk off the coast of Unalaska Island, Alaska, during a rescue. The Jayhawk was sent to a sinking cargo ship, the *Selendang Ayu*, and was in the process of airlifting the crew. The rescue swimmer had been deployed directly onto the cargo ship. Six sailors were safely hoisted to the helicopter, and a seventh was being brought up in the basket when disaster struck. A rogue wave caught the pilots unaware and engulfed the helicopter in spray and water, causing the engine to stall. The helicopter tumbled down, where it clipped the side of the ship and fell into the sea. The three-person helicopter crew all managed to extricate themselves from the wreck. With the aid of their dry suits, they stayed alive until another helicopter rescued them and the one survivor being hoisted at the time of the crash. The six sailors who had been airlifted into the Jayhawk perished.

The rescue swimmer and the ship's captain were still on board the cargo ship, and the seas tore that in two before the second helicopter rescued them.

~

All four of the crewmen flying out to the *Sean Seamour II* are dressed in the same dry suits that helped save the crew of the helicopter that crashed in the Alaska accident. A dry suit is required whenever crew members operate over waters colder than seventy degrees. If they crash into the water, these suits have seals at the ends of the arms and legs to help the crew fight off hypothermia. Though the suits do breathe a bit, they can make the men uncomfortably hot while flying, especially if they pick up hypothermic survivors who need the helicopter's heater at its maximum temperature. Drew and Scott, who will be doing the most physical kind of work, will feel as if they are in a sauna if they need to blast the heater for chilled survivors.

The suits are bright orange, except for the one worn by Scott Higgins, whose green flight suit is an indication of his other duties as an aerial precision marksman. The thirty-three-year-old six-footer with black hair is somewhat unusual in that he is both a flight engineer and marksman. His role as flight engineer/hoist operator is to save lives, while his role as a Coast Guard marksman is to kill anyone who threatens the lives of American citizens or elected officials.

Scott has participated in many rescues, and he has learned to expect the unexpected. Now, as he and his fellow crew members launch for the long flight to the *Sean Seamour II,* he starts playing different scenarios in his mind, reminding himself that there is nothing routine when a rescue takes place this far offshore.

TETHER OURSELVES
TOGETHER

Drowning and hypothermia are the first two obstacles that JP, Rudy, and Ben will have to overcome to stay alive through the day. Not far off, however, will be two new challenges: sharks and dehydration. With the surface of the ocean in such a chaotic state, sharks in the area are probably staying well below the crashing waves. But as soon as the seas abate, the life raft will attract them like a magnet. In a section of ocean devoid of floating objects, a life raft is a curiosity for sharks, and they will come to investigate.

Colors also draw sharks, particularly bright colors. Dark hues, such as deep blue and black, are the least appealing. So while life rafts need to be a bright color for planes, helicopters, and boats to spot, that same feature increases the odds of the life raft being visited by sharks. The bottom part of JP's life raft—all that is left—is black, but a couple of tattered slices of the orange canopy trail off its side.

Because sharks can sense vibrations in the water, a person moving or bailing inside the life raft is sending out a signal to sharks that seems to say, "Come here. There is something alive and wounded." Large sharks, such as blues, makos, and great whites, fear nothing and are lured in by the sounds and motion and, eventually, the sight of something large and unusual in the ocean. A shark may find a meal in the form of other fish swimming beneath the raft. Maybe it's the raft's color or the shade or shelter it provides, but bait fish often fin beneath it. This in turn attracts larger fish, and those get the attention of sharks. And once the sharks linger, they are sure to know that something is alive inside the raft.

Curiously, instead of attacking with their teeth, most sharks, upon first encountering a raft, "bump" the vessel. These bumps can be in the form of a gentle nudge or a rubbing of the shark's back along the entire length of the raft. Perhaps sharks use bumping as a cautious way to probe the raft to sense what's inside, or, with harder blows, to knock its contents into the sea. The bumps and blows may escalate to attacks if a shark sees there is a living creature—food—inside the raft.

Laura Hillenbrand, in her book *Unbroken*, describes how Louis Zamparini and two other castaways in a life raft were being circled and nudged by sharks until Louie leaned over the edge of the raft. One of the sharks "leapt from the water at a terrific speed, mouth wide open, lunging straight at his head." Louie lifted his hands in front of his face and managed to push and turn the shark just before it took his head in its mouth.

Later in his ordeal, Louie encountered a different kind of assault by a shark, this one by a twenty-foot-long great white that sped up from the depths, crashed into the raft, and sent it airborne. Somehow all three castaways managed to stay inside, so the shark tried knocking them out with its tail. It was only after several harrowing tail slaps against the raft that the shark glided away.

A similar experience happened to Bill and Simonne Butler, husband and wife, who drifted in the Pacific in a leaky life raft after their boat was sunk by a pod of pilot whales. In Bill's book, *66 Days Adrift*, he describes how medium-sized sharks "punched, shoved, and knocked" their raft throughout an entire night, causing him to wonder how much punishment the raft could take. The raft was tested by sharks—perhaps the same ones—many more nights, but Bill and Simonne were able to patch small leaks, keeping it afloat. A new problem occurred when the sharks left. Bill caught some fish to eat and threw the carcasses overboard, where triggerfish ate them. A few minutes later, Bill wondered why the triggerfish scattered when he threw fish guts into the sea. He peered into the ocean and learned why: "A great white shark with a head two feet in diameter" was under the raft. The great white stayed with the raft for the entire day, and as nightfall closed in, the raft was violently spun around 180 degrees. Bill feared it was the great white, but as he squinted into the dusk, he was "met with one of the happiest sights I have ever seen": a group of smaller sharks was near the raft, which meant the great white had moved on.

~

For now JP, Rudy, and Ben keep their worries about sharks in check, knowing that first the raft must stay in one piece throughout the storm. They have no idea how long the un-named storm will last, but already they're moderately thirsty and rue the fact that the survival bag is at the bottom of the ocean instead of in the raft. All three men have been expend-ing energy fighting the sea. Even when they're not moving, they are losing internal water through the vapor they exhale just by breathing. JP in particular did so many tasks and put forth so much effort on the *Sean Seamour II* that he should have been hydrating himself frequently before he abandoned ship. But there was so much happening, so many decisions, and so much pain from the broken ribs that drinking water was the last thing on his mind.

There is no freshwater, and sipping seawater, even a few drops, is out of the question. The sodium in salt water must be removed by urinating, which causes the loss of even more fluid.

And drinking large amounts of seawater will lead to death, as it pulls moisture out of brain cells, leading to hallucinations while increasing the rate of dehydration.

JP will be the first of the three to feel the effects of dehydration, because he is already suffering from hypothermia and shock. Indeed, mild dehydration may have played a role in the convulsions he suffered earlier. The initial effects of dehydration include light-headedness, lethargy, muscle cramps, and confusion. As the dehydration worsens, it can lead to seizures, heart palpitations, and eventual unconsciousness. A dehydrated person's blood vessels constrict to compensate for the loss of fluid in the blood in order to maintain blood pressure for vital organs. The reaction is similar to what happens with hypothermia, where blood is restricted to the outer extremities so that vital organs can function. Because JP is suffering from both problems, he is getting a double dose of trouble. He needs to get warm and hydrated, fast.

JP continues to come in and out of consciousness. He has watched the near-vertical walls of water assault the raft and believes that the storm will last a lot longer than he can hang on. He thinks of Rudy's age—sixty-two—and knows that his odds of survival aren't much better. Maybe Ben, only thirty-one, will have the stamina to outlast the storm and stay alive long enough to be found. That's a long shot, and JP knows it, so he tugs on Rudy's rain gear and says, "Maybe we should all tether ourselves together."

Rudy and Ben are surprised to hear JP talk, but they

understand what he's saying. They know he means that if they tether themselves to one another and then to the raft, there will be a better chance that their bodies will be found.

"I was thinking the same thing," says Rudy, his voice trailing off. He knows it will be easier on the families if their bodies are recovered.

~

As the Jayhawk launches, Commander Nevada Smith, Copilot Aaron Nelson, Rescue Swimmer Drew Dazzo, and Flight Mechanic Scott Higgins settle in for the 250-mile flight. It will take about an hour and forty-five minutes. The first hundred miles are rough, but nothing Scott hasn't flown through in the past. They're cruising between five hundred and nine hundred feet above the ocean, through rain and wind gusts of forty-five knots. Visibility is between a quarter and a half mile, and the flight is below cloud cover. It's hard to judge the height of the waves at this altitude, without any boats or structures in the water for context, but Scott guesses they are about twenty feet.

Drew is also keeping an eye on the waves below, and though he guesses they're fifteen to twenty feet high, he notes the amount of white water and figures that the interval between waves is short and that each wave is steep enough to be breaking. He is also listening to Nevada and Aaron on the radio as they keep everyone apprised of the climbing wind speeds.

"We've got gusts of fifty," says Nevada. A few minutes later, "Gusts have climbed to sixty."

The helicopter is being bumped and buffeted, making the ride uncomfortable, and it is far from the storm's center. Sometimes it gets pushed from side to side; sometimes it drops and rises abruptly. The pilots begin to alter course slightly whenever they encounter the most severe squalls. Drew hears the C-130 commander over the radio, giving them directions on the best altitudes. He also hears Nevada and Aaron calling out wind gusts of eighty knots. *That's unbelievable*, Drew thinks. Being a swimmer, he tries to imagine the state of the ocean in the face of such winds. He doesn't like the picture beginning to form.

Although the C-130 is reporting such dangerous wind speeds, Drew is comforted to hear the voice of the airplane's commander. If the C-130 crew can spot the boat in trouble or the people in the water, Drew knows he can get right to work without having to wait through the search part of the SAR. He also knows he will have another set of eyes looking down on him when he begins the rescue. The C-130 crew members are his angels, men and women who look after him if some-thing goes wrong on the helicopter. They won't be able to extract him from the ocean, but they'll be above him with the ability to drop survival equipment, and that's reassuring when treading water alone far out to sea.

Drew is getting himself psyched for the rescue, as an ath-lete would before a big game. He's got the butterflies in his stomach that he always gets when he knows the conditions are bad. It's a feeling he relishes; it means his adrenaline is on standby. He's got a hunch that this rescue will be one of his more difficult attempts, and he quickly runs through trouble he might expect, recalling other SARs he performed.

The thirty-four-year-old has been in the Coast Guard for eight years, and unlike some of his peers, he did not dream of being a rescue swimmer; he chose the career path after trying other work.

Drew grew up in Ridge, a town on Long Island in New York, and was one of those kids who could never sit still. He always wanted to be outside doing something—racing BMX bicycles and dirt bikes or playing soccer, hockey, or volleyball. Although he was never on his high school swim team, he spent a lot of time on the ocean, using a small family boat for fishing trips and waterskiing. After he finished high school, he wasn't sure what he wanted to do, so he took the first job offered to him, as a carpenter hired to frame houses.

He swung a hammer for the next several years. Then, when he was twenty-five, he and his parents visited the Intrepid Sea, Air & Space Museum in New York City. The Coast Guard was also there, putting on a demonstration off the stern of the aircraft carrier. Drew watched with fascination as a boat dropped someone in the water, then a helicopter swooped in and a rescue swimmer leaped out and went through a mock rescue. Right then and there, Drew had an epiphany. He turned to his father and said, "I want to be that rescue swimmer." He finally knew what he wanted to do with his life. Reaching his goal would take a lot more than desire and hard work, though. It would require a single-minded, all-consuming quest and a real gut check of his mental and physical stamina.

First he went to the Coast Guard recruiting office and passed the physical. His background check turned up a DUI (driving under the influence of alcohol) charge, and the recruiter told him that the black mark on his record might be insurmountable.

Drew wrote a series of essays about why he would be a good addition to the Coast Guard, but they weren't enough. He added recommendations from all the adults who knew him, along with a letter from his congressman. Finally, just after his twenty-sixth birthday, Drew was accepted and began his three months of boot camp in Cape May. Upon completion, each new member was allowed to request where he or she would like to be stationed. Drew wanted to get as far away from New York as possible and be close to a wilderness area. On his selection sheet for a station, he wrote "anywhere in Alaska."

The Coast Guard was happy to oblige. Drew was sent to Sitka, where he served on a buoy tender, a ship used to service buoys. As soon as he achieved the required six months of service, he submitted his name for rescue swimmer school. Only a handful of hopeful candidates are accepted, and of those who do, just a small percentage graduate. (There are only about three hundred rescue swimmers, formally known as aviation survival technicians [ASTs], in the entire Coast Guard.)

Drew had an eighteen-month wait in Sitka before he was allowed to compete for one of the coveted rescue swimmer positions. During that time, his life and responsibilities changed significantly from his days as a carefree house framer. He fell in love, married, and became a stepfather to his wife's daughter from a previous marriage.

When Drew finally began the first phase of his quest to become a rescue swimmer, he was, at twenty-eight, one of the older candidates. He initially went through the rigors of the four-month AST training program, and then it was on to another four months of training at AST A-School, held at Elizabeth City. (Only about seventy-five candidates are accepted to the school, and the training is on par with the difficulty of what Army Rangers, Navy SEALs, and Air Force Pararescue jumpers must endure.) At A-School, instructors want to see how candidates respond in various water drills under stressful situations. The goal is to push the trainees to their limits and beyond so that only the most committed men or women are left. (Women undergo the same training and tests as men; there are currently three active female rescue swimmers.) About half the trainees wash out of this part of the program. Those who make it are then sent to emergency medical technician training school, and upon successful completion, they're admitted into the apprentice program at one of the Coast Guard air stations.

Like all the other candidates, Drew found the process extremely demanding. Prior to being admitted to the program, he put himself on a grueling daily exercise regimen so he could be as prepared as possible. He knew that only the Coasties in great physical shape sign up to become rescue swimmers, and he also was aware the instructors would drive them all to the breaking point. Drew needed to be his strongest and fastest, but also to develop a stamina that few people have. While all that preparation helped, A-School required him to dig much deeper and draw on a mental toughness he wasn't aware he had.

The water drills, particularly the buddy swim and the "bullpen" session, challenged Drew's endurance. In the buddy swim, he had to drag a person eight hundred meters (about a half mile) without stopping to rest. The bullpen session is even worse. In that drill, six instructors encircle the rescue swimmer and, one at a time, act like a panicked, drowning person—tugging, hugging, clawing, and pulling the rescue swimmer down. The swimmer must somehow break their grip without punching them in the head, while still getting enough air to keep from drowning.

Drew was able to perform better than most of the candidates in these water drills, but he found the long-distance runs to be difficult. Equally tough was being away from his wife and daughter for several months.

Upon Drew's graduation, he was fortunate to be stationed in Hawaii. It was there that he performed his first rescue: saving his own daughter. He and his family were at the beach when his daughter, at age six, got caught in a rip current. She screamed for help.

Drew went after her, and by the time he caught up, they were seventy-five yards out. He told her to ride on his back. He then did the breaststroke, swimming parallel to the shore. He could feel the pull of the rip, and he kept as much of his body near the surface as possible because riptides are stronger deep down. After about five minutes, he felt the current release them, and he was able to head in.

That rescue meant the world to Drew. There was no helicopter, no free-fall jump, and no hoist, but his daughter was safe, and Drew knew it was because of his training.

For the four and a half years that Drew was in Hawaii, the water rescue of his daughter turned out to be the only one he performed. He had plenty of medevacs (medical evacuations) of injured people off vessels, but not the water rescues he had trained so hard for. He even began hoping the SAR alarm would send out its piercing warble so he could be dropped into the ocean.

His next station assignment was Elizabeth City, and he decided to stop obsessing about water rescues. As soon as he put rescues out of his mind, the cases started coming in whenever he was on duty. His fellow rescue swimmers began to notice. The swimmers are a tight-knit group, and they have their own "shop," where one of them is always stationed by a phone, radio, or computer to monitor any potential SARs. The other swimmers are either working out or organizing rescue equipment, from dry suits to parachutes to life rafts. Hanging on the walls of the equipment room, up near the ceiling, are life vests worn by the people saved by the rescue swimmers.

Written on each PFD in marker pen is the name of the survivor, the vessel, the date of the rescue, and the name of the rescue swimmer.

Soon Drew's name appeared on several PFDs, and the newer swimmers would ask, "Why is it you're getting so many rescues?" Drew would smile and say, "Good things happen to those who wait."

And now Drew is flying over two hundred miles out to sea for yet another SAR, and he thinks, *I'm not even supposed to be the backup rescue swimmer.* The day before, a fellow rescue swimmer was incarcerated in the county jail after getting into an altercation at a bar. Drew spent much of the day figuring out the legal process of getting his friend released and working with a bail bondsman. The arrested rescue swimmer was scheduled to stand duty as a backup swimmer that night, but a superior didn't think it was a good idea. So Drew volunteered to be the backup. That night he tuned in to the TV weather report and heard about the potential for high winds. He wasn't surprised when the phone rang at five a.m. and he was told he was needed at the station ASAP.

~

Drew gazes out the window of the helicopter, then looks at Scott, who has been doing the same. It's hard to tell, but the waves now look to be forty feet high. Both men have done all sorts of difficult water rescues, but neither has done one in seas this large. And they still have another half hour of flying southeast into the storm, into the Gulf Stream.

16

"MARK, MARK, MARK!"

It is seven a.m., and the C-130 is below cloud cover, being buffeted and blasted by eighty-knot winds. Copilot Edward Ahlstrand sits next to Aircraft Commander Paul Beavis, and both are in absolute awe of what they see below. Ahlstrand knows he is witnessing waves of a magnitude he will never see again. He expected bad conditions, but this is something else entirely. Even the color of the ocean is different from anything he's encountered. There is an absence of blue; instead, an endless succession of gray, green, and white water is churning, crashing, and shooting spray into the air.

The plane's radar can do 270-degree sweeps of the water and should be able to pick out a boat and maybe a raft on the ocean. It also has the potential to pick out a person in the water, but not in these conditions. Ahlstrand hopes the EPIRB came from a boat—he knows how difficult it would be for the radar or the human eye to locate a life raft, and nearly impossible to find a person. Marcus Jones, the navigator, is thinking the same thing. They have already been flying racetrack-pattern loops over the last known position of the EPIRB hit. *If anyone is in a raft or the water, being tumbled by those waves,* thinks Jones, *they are probably already dead.*

Suddenly, Jones sits up straight, eyes wide. He thought he heard a faint tone from an electronic signal. He sits motionless, straining to listen through his headset. He hears it again. "Just heard a faint signal!" he shouts. "Probably an EPIRB. Let's go back!" At the same instant, he notices a tiny blip on the radar. Then it disappears. He prays it is not just debris.

The plane is moving between 150 and 170 knots per hour, approximately two and a half to three miles per minute. It will be tough to see anything with the naked eye, and Jones is hoping the radar will pick up something on the next pass. The pilots bank the plane, turning in a wide arc back toward the EPIRB hit, flying at just four hundred feet above the ocean. As the C-130 zooms past the location of the signal, Jones is focused on the radar, and the other six crew members are searching the ocean for anything other than water. But neither the radar nor the crew locate any objects in the tempest below. Jones shakes his head. *We are in the right area; where are they?*

Rudy and Ben see the plane at the same time. They're down in a trough, looking up at a patch of sky framed on either side by moving walls of green water. For a brief moment, the plane speeds into view, the orange Coast Guard stripe on its side clearly visible. The wind and waves are so loud they can barely hear the roar of its engines. The plane is about three hundred yards off to the left and seems to fly a few feet above the seas. Just as quickly, the aircraft is out of sight, blocked by the nearest wave. Both men are too stunned to say a word, and they are barely able to hold back their tears of joy. They think the Coast Guard crew in the plane got a good look at them because they were so close.

JP is conscious and surprises his friends by croaking, "They know we are here. . . ." He, too, saw the plane for an instant before it streaked behind the towering waves.

"Yes!" shouts Rudy. "They found us!"

Minutes go by—they feel like an eternity. Then the plane appears again. It is still off to the left. Rudy begins to worry. *Maybe they didn't see us. They must have got our original emergency signal, but maybe don't know exactly where we are.*

Quickly, he yanks one of the flares he had stuck in the pocket of his raincoat right before exiting the boat. The protective cover must be pulled off and then used to strike the head of the flare to ignite it, similar to lighting a match. The ten-inch handheld flare, once lit, will shoot out a bright flame. Try as he might, Rudy cannot get the flare to light. He curses, tosses it into the ocean, and desperately pulls another one from his pocket. He curses to himself as he strikes it with the cap. He uses all his strength, striking the flare again and again, but nothing will make it light. Shaking with frustration and anger, he hurls this one into the ocean as well, fearing that the C-130 has left for good.

"Have you got any more?" Ben shouts. A particularly large wave bears down on the tiny vessel. Luckily, its sheer wall does not collapse, and it slides beneath the raft.

Rudy digs deep into his pocket and pulls out the last flare. This one is a rocket flare, larger than the others. Rudy is trying to calm himself, but he's got no time to lose. He aims the flare's cylinder-shaped tube directly above the raft and, holding his breath, pulls the string that acts as the trigger.

The flare hisses and then fires upward, a bright orange ball of flame heading toward the gray sky. It is designed to go several hundred feet into the air, but it travels only about fifty feet, then is caught by the wind and blown sideways into a wave. *Oh God,* thinks Rudy, *the plane can't have seen it.*

~

"Mark! Mark! Mark!" shouts Marcus Jones. He has moved away from the radar screen to a window and, out of the corner of his eye, spots a glowing streak of orange. He wants the crew to mark the aircraft's position so they can circle back to the exact spot where he saw the light.

Beavis and Ahlstrand put the plane into a steep bank and

complete the semicircle bringing them back to the mark. All seven crew members stare out the windows, expecting to see a boat just ahead. But at 150 miles per hour, they get only a quick glimpse of the area. All they see is slashing rain pelting the windows, and acres of towering white peaks and dark gray valleys below.

Jones waits at the window as the pilots bank the plane once again. He knows what he saw, and it was most definitely a flare. *Where did the boat disappear to? Could it have sunk in just the few minutes since I saw the streak of light? Could it have drifted well beyond the initial mark?*

Beavis speaks through the headsets. "Okay, we are almost back at the marked spot." Jones is at the window, looking a short distance ahead of the plane. He sees something that makes him gasp. A tiny black object, which appears to be the size of a dime, is halfway up the face of a wind-streaked wave. "A raft!" he shouts. "Two o'clock on our right! I think at least one person is on it!"

Some of the others in the plane see it as well, and then, just like that, it's gone from sight. Jones thinks, *That raft didn't even seem inflated. How in the world could anyone stay on it? It was tiny. Maybe it wasn't even a raft but debris from the boat, with one or more persons hanging on to it.*

Now the rest of the crew gets busy. In the cargo area is something called an MA-3 kit. It is made up of five canvas bags, each about the size of a small trash barrel. In three of the bags are life rafts that will start to inflate as soon as they leave the aircraft. In the remaining two bags are survival supplies, such as food, water, whistles, reflecting mirrors, and sunscreen. The bags are stretched out along fifteen hundred feet of line, so there is a better chance that part of the line will be near the survivors. Normally, this is what would be dropped out the rear cargo door, but Commander Beavis is having second thoughts. With hurricane-force winds, he is not sure how far off course the kit will be blown before reaching the water. He also worries that if the survivors leave their partially inflated raft to try to swim to another that is twenty to thirty feet away, they will drown before they reach it. He decides they will drop one raft and see what happens.

Through his headset, Beavis tells Casey Green and Ryan Cantu to get ready with a single raft, adding, "In seas this big, the survivors might be better off staying with their own raft unless we can put one right next to them. After you drop our raft, let me know how far from the survivors it lands. We may want to save our other rafts until the survivors' raft starts sinking further or is torn apart."

Green acknowledges the instructions and begins to position a single raft at the rear of the plane. It's not an easy job. The back of the aircraft takes the full brunt of the extreme turbulence, shuddering as if the hand of a giant is shaking it. The drop master fights back motion sickness, then opens the cargo door and waits for the plane to circle back toward the survivors.

The other scanners in the plane tell Green they're almost

above the survivors. Peering out the cargo door, he soon sees the survivors below and aft of the aircraft and quickly launches his raft. The raft is immediately taken by the wind and seems to be blown horizontally, pushed well to the right of the survivors. With all the foam on the surface of the ocean, it's hard to see exactly where it lands, but the drop master knows it never got near the survivors.

Beavis and Ahlstrand bank the plane once again and return to the spot where the survivors were seen. The raft is gone! Not one of the seven crew members can see it. Ahlstrand is thinking, *We can't lose sight of them now. If we can't find them on our next pass, we may have lost them for good.*

Again they make the loop back to the location, factoring in the raft's quick drift rate, and this time half the crew sees the black raft below. Ahlstrand lets out a sigh of relief. He knows the waves must have blocked the survivors from view and realizes what a challenge it will be not to lose them in the chaos below.

Beavis is on the radio to SAR Headquarters. "We have spotted a life raft, or a makeshift life raft, with survivors. Not sure how many, but we think we saw two people. We have dropped a raft, but it was blown away. We will attempt to keep the survivors in sight for the Jayhawk. Tell the [helicopter] crew that visibility is fair to poor, wind gusts just above eighty knots, and the waves are enormous! We have enough fuel to stay on scene for another five hours."

Commander Beavis gives their location, then signs off. He

and his crew have shifted out of the search mode and are going to do their best not to lose visual sight of the target. The pilot and copilot alternate time at the aircraft's controls to ward off fatigue brought on by the extreme flying conditions. It is impossible to keep the plane in any type of steady flight; the altitude indicators are in a constant state of flux, rocking and vacillating wildly. The pilots decide to deploy two flares the next time they pass the raft to help mark its location. These flares, which are water-activated, emit a solid trail of white smoke that on most days can be seen at a great distance and help aircrews visually relocate targets in the water. On this day, the flares and their smoke trails simply vanish, absorbed by the white froth covering the ocean. Beavis knows if they can't keep a visual on the raft when they pass overhead, the men in the water will die.

~

At SAR Headquarters, Supervisor Geoff Pagels communicates with Beavis. He now knows they have a real emergency with people in a raft associated with the first EPIRB activated, the one registered to a vessel named *Lou Pantai* (actually, the *Sean Seamour II*). The C-130 will stay on scene, which means he needs to call Elizabeth City and have a crew for another C-130 assemble to investigate the EPIRB signal from the *Flying Colours*. Pagels has recently gotten a good location fix for that EPIRB from a passing satellite.

The contact for the men in the raft is Betty de Lutz, and Pagels has promised her that he will call as soon as he has new information. When he gets Betty on the phone, he says, "Our search plane has located a life raft. We now have to wait for our helicopter to get on scene for the rescue. The crew of our aircraft tell me there are perhaps two survivors on board."

"No!" Betty shouts. "There were three people on the boat!"

"Okay," says Pagels, "I understand. I'll be sure to tell the pilots to look for three people. I will call you back as soon as I have more news."

Pagels alerts both the helicopter and C-130 pilots that there should be three people on the raft. Then he gets back on the phone, still trying to make connection with the listed numbers for the EPIRB of the *Flying Colours* to confirm that the vessel is out at sea. While punching in phone numbers, he wonders, *What kind of storm is this that so many vessels are in trouble?*

LIKE A HOCKEY PUCK ON ICE

The excitement of seeing the C–130 does not last long for Ben. About every five or ten minutes, it zips briefly into view between the passing waves. JP has slipped back into unconsciousness, but Ben and Rudy have talked a little. Both have come to the conclusion that the winds are too much for a helicopter to fly in, and that the C–130 is just trying to keep track of their position. Ben thinks that by the time the storm abates enough for a helicopter to launch, he will be dead.

Time drags on. For the next two hours, the plane circles while the men below do their best to stay with the raft. It seems the raft is riding lower in the water and might have a leak, but it's impossible to know for sure or to find the source of any escaping air. It barely matters if the raft is right side up or upside down; in both positions, it's like sitting in the middle of a trampoline filled with water.

~

Aboard the C–130 aircraft, Commander Beavis gives Jayhawk helicopter pilot Nevada Smith the coordinates and drift rate of the raft. Both Nevada and his copilot, Aaron Nelson, are elated: they won't have to waste precious fuel and time searching. Nevada plugs the coordinates into the aircraft navigation system and establishes a point where they can intercept the raft.

Aaron estimates that they'll have close to one hour to perform the rescue. *We have time,* Aaron thinks, *and that means everything, with conditions this bad.*

When the helicopter pilots are near where they expect the raft to be, they descend to three hundred feet. They hold in a hover, scanning the seas. All they can see is wave after towering wave. Wind blasts rock the helicopter every which way, putting the pilot on edge. Nevada is so awestruck by the maelstrom below that he picks up his video camera and films the scene.

Scott opens up the aircraft doorway, and the wailing wind whips through the cabin with a strange sucking sound. Drew and Scott are on their bellies, and they slide to the open door and poke their heads out. The sensation is similar to sticking your head out the sunroof of a race car going 150 miles per hour. The view is like looking down on the Swiss Alps—snowcapped summits and dark valleys. But these mountains are moving, all advancing in the same direction.

Over the radio, Nevada contacts Beavis, saying, "We still can't see them."

Beavis, circling the C-130 above the Jayhawk, answers, "Follow me. We're about to go right over them."

Scott, hanging his head out the doorway, instinctively flinches as he sees the C-130 pass close by.

The C-130 roars a couple hundred feet past the HH-60 Jayhawk. Rain splatters on the helicopter's windshield in such volume that the wipers have a hard time keeping up. Nevada watches the C-130 bank hard.

"Hey, Nevada," says Beavis, "they're off our wing right now." Nevada and the crew look into the white-and-gray mess below.

"Still don't see them," says Nevada.

"Turn to two o'clock. Do you see them now?" asks Beavis.

"No."

"You're almost directly over them. Look forward just a bit and off to your right."

Nevada looks at an oncoming wave. About halfway up the wave is a small black object. *Whoa!* thinks Nevada, *these waves are even bigger than I thought. They must be eighty feet!* The eight-foot life raft is the first thing to contrast with the waves, and it looks minuscule compared to the towering seas. Imagine the wave is the size of notebook paper. Now imagine the raft is the size of a small button, no more than a quarter inch across. That is what Nevada is seeing, and it makes him gasp, especially when the top part of the wave—fifteen feet of churning white water—bears down on the raft.

Scott and Drew, squinting into the windblown rain, see the raft a second or two after the pilots do, and their initial impression is the same as Nevada's: the waves are unlike anything they have ever seen. Scott thinks, *Oh my God. These waves are triple the size I guessed earlier. The raft is just flying along—it's doing over six knots. This won't be easy. How in the hell are we ever going to do this?* He sees a wave break, and he tries to imagine being slammed under by the avalanching water. *If I get buried by one of those, it's going to push me down like a sledgehammer.* He begins to consider how long it will take to claw back to the surface, then shakes his head. *Do not think about it. Stay positive. You can do this.*

Nevada is back on the radio to Beavis. "Okay, we see it. Looks like there are two or maybe three people on the raft." To Aaron, sitting next to him, he says, "Can you believe this?"

"It's unreal," Aaron answers.

"I've never seen waves like this, not even close. The raft looks like a hockey puck on ice, the way it's moving."

Beavis breaks in. "Okay, we will be circling above you at sixteen hundred feet." The commander of the C-130 climbs to sixteen hundred feet, where the plane will be better able to conserve fuel and stay at a safe distance from the Jayhawk

Aaron, who is doing most of the flying, lowers the

helicopter to 120 feet above the cavernous wave troughs. The circulating air from the rotor wash makes the water below them look like a blizzard. Aaron has the helicopter's nose into the wind, which uses the least amount of power in a hover. He manages power by a lever to his left, a collective, and he controls direction via a lever directly in front of him and extending up between his legs, a cyclic.

Nevada conns Aaron—that is, he gives Aaron directional instructions to position the aircraft—to a point directly behind the raft, and they hold there to allow Scott and Drew to get ready for the deployment. At this low altitude, the crew has a much better view of the half-submerged black raft, and they can see that there are three people hanging on to it.

Nevada alerts Beavis on the C-130, saying, "We've got a good look at the raft, and there are three people. Two are wearing yellow gear, but one [Ben] is in dark red and hard to pick out from the raft. That's why you couldn't see him. Our flight mechanic and swimmer are getting ready, and we'll try to do a basket hoist." He turns to Aaron. "Can we get a little lower?"

"Roger."

The copilot lowers the helicopter another twenty feet.

Despite the swirling foam and spray, Drew can see the wave tops clearly. He thinks he can save time by going into the water without the cable if he times his jump into the highest point of the wave. Through his headset, he says to Nevada, "Can we do a free-fall deployment?"

"Do you really think that's the safest way to enter the water?" asks Nevada, trying to tamp down Drew's adrenaline.

Drew rethinks his approach. "You're right. I'll go down on the strop [a slinglike device]."

Nevada knows that rescue swimmers live for this kind of moment and that Drew would jump into a volcano if necessary. He also knows the risks. The rescue swimmer can lose his mask or a fin, or a survivor can choke him. And the swimmer will most definitely be ingesting seawater and working in a state of near exhaustion. In fact, Nevada considers the rescue swimmer another PIW (person in water) who could be in an emergency situation of his own. The commander takes that a step further and considers that the operation will have a total of six rescues/hoists: the three people on the raft plus three times hoisting Drew. (The rescue swimmer will need to be retrieved after getting each survivor in the basket, because the raft will have blown far away, and the swimmer will need to be brought back up and then repositioned for the next drop. The basket is too small to bring up both Drew and a survivor at the same time.)

Suddenly, Aaron says, "Did you see that?"

"What?" says Nevada.

"The radar altimeter (which measures how far the helicopter is from the ocean) just went from a hundred to twenty."

"Incredible."

"That's an eighty-foot wave!"

"I'll start calling out the big waves."

Aaron knows Scott will need the helicopter to be as low as possible to hoist the survivors, but the copilot has made up his mind that his top objective will be to provide a margin of safety between the aircraft and any rogue waves. *Just listen to Nevada, do what Scott says, and keep an eye on the second wave crest coming at us.* There is so much going on that Aaron needs to keep it simple. *Stay relaxed; we have time. Take it slow. If it takes more than one attempt to get the first man, that's okay.*

Aaron has his priorities, and number one is to avoid having a wave sneak up on him and clip the underside of the helicopter. With waves this big, that's a real possibility, and if that happens, it's all over for both survivors and aircrew.

DEPLOYING THE SWIMMER

J P's stepmother is pacing the floor of her Cape Cod home. She has been up half the night, ever since the first call from the Coast Guard. Now she has just received a call from the Coast Guard saying they have spotted a life raft.

Betty has a difficult decision to make. Should she call JP's wife, Mayke, to let her know that the *Sean Seamour II* sank in a storm and a Coast Guard plane has spotted a raft? Mayke surely deserves to know what is happening, but Betty hesitates because of the reference the Coast Guard contact made in the last conversation to two people in the raft rather than three. That sent a chill up Betty's spine and prompted her to pray harder. *What if one of the men is dead and swept away? It could be*

JP. . . . I won't call Mayke until I know for certain whether JP is dead or alive. And if he's alive, I won't call until I can tell her if he is okay or injured.

Betty is startled out of her ruminations by the ringing telephone. Instead of picking it up on the first ring, she says a quick prayer. Then she answers the phone.

"Mrs. de Lutz, this is Geoff Pagels from the Coast Guard."

"Yes. Tell me what is happening."

"We now have a helicopter at the emergency scene, in addition to an orbiting C-130 plane. The helicopter pilots were able to get low enough to see clearly into the life raft."

Betty doesn't breathe. The next sentence means everything.

"The pilots tell us there are three people in the raft. They are just about to lower the rescue swimmer. Once they do that, they will begin hoisting the survivors up."

"So they are alive?"

"We think so. At least one is alive, because a flare was fired from the raft, so chances are the others are alive as well. But this is a bad storm. These are experienced pilots, and they have never seen waves like the ones on scene."

"What else can you tell me?"

"That's all we know. But as soon as I learn more, I'll call you."

"Thank you. Thank you so much," says Betty, her voice trailing off. She sits heavily in a chair, drained of energy but relieved. *I'm not going to call Mayke until that man calls me back and says JP is alive and well and in the helicopter.*

Betty has no idea that across the ocean on a hilltop in France, Mayke is in her studio, staring into space, unable to paint, because she has an unshakable feeling that something awful has happened to JP.

~

JP, slumped in Rudy's arms, is unconscious, totally unaware of the image appearing above him. From seemingly out of nowhere, a helicopter is hovering directly overhead, its rotor wash sending out circular bands of spray snatched up from the ocean. Rudy is so startled that he thinks maybe he's hallucinating. The helicopter is just a hundred feet overhead. He can see the orange Coast Guard stripe and the open cabin door.

Ben, too, is caught off guard. The waves surrounding them are so tall that he could not see the helicopter approach and could not hear its engine above the blasting wind. Now the sight of this giant steel aircraft so near their little raft is more than he can process. It's a surreal experience, as if he's watching a movie about someone else's life and rescue. But the helicopter stays in place, and Ben knows it's real. He feels euphoric. Just a minute earlier, he had no hope and was waiting for the inevitable conclusion. Now salvation has come down out of the clouds. He also wonders how in the world the rescuers will get them off the raft with three-story waves crashing and colliding all around.

~

Rescue swimmer Drew Dazzo checks his dry suit one last time, making sure the seals are tight. He tells the others he's going off the internal communication system. He removes his headset and puts on his fins, mask and snorkel, and gloves, and finally his neon-yellow rescue helmet.

He and Scott have talked about the rescue steps. Because the raft is moving so fast, Scott has told Drew not to even try to get back to the raft after the first survivor is in the basket. Instead, Scott will lower the strop and Drew can put the sling around his chest. Then Scott can either ferry Drew to the raft without him returning to the helicopter or, if the raft has moved a great distance, bring Drew back up and redeploy when the pilots relocate the raft.

Scott motions for Drew to come to the door, and the rescue swimmer moves into a sitting position at the edge of the doorframe. Scott hands him the hook and strop, and Drew secures the nylon sling under his arms. While all this is going on, Scott is letting the pilots know exactly what is happening, painting a verbal picture of the action, using scripted language. It's imperative that everything Scott says through his headset is clear and precise because he will also do the conning so the swimmer can be lowered as close as possible to the raft.

Scott is wearing leather gloves so he won't cut his hands on the cable. In his right hand is a pendant attached to a long wire cord that controls the hoist, which is suspended from a steel arm extending from the airframe above the door. Scott also has on a thick belt connected to a safety strap fixed to the rear wall of the helicopter cabin. Because Scott will be spending a fair amount of time leaning out of the aircraft, the belt and strap will keep him from tumbling into the sea.

Scott is in a kneeling position and cranes his head out the doorway to get a better look at the raft and the waves. The wind snatches the breath right out of him. In all his prior rescues, the wind never exceeded thirty knots, and now he's being blasted by eighty- to eighty-five-knot gusts. It's impossible to talk, and he's winded within a minute. He gets a good look at the waves and notices that every third one is a bit bigger than the two before it. He's trying to get a feel for the seas and wants to be sure that he times Drew's descent so the swimmer isn't going into one of the larger waves.

Nevada gives the go-ahead for deployment. Scott taps Drew on the chest, the signal that he is ready. Drew gives his partner the thumbs-up sign that he, too, is ready to be lowered and begin the rescue.

"Deploying the swimmer."

Using the pendant, Scott pulls up a bit of cable while Drew leans out the doorway until he is in the air. Scott puts a hand on Drew to keep him from being blown back into the airframe, and then he slowly releases cable and Drew starts his descent.

"Swimmer is outside the cabin. Swimmer is being lowered."

Drew is amazed by the power of the wind pushing him back toward the rear of the aircraft. A strap from his mask is hitting his helmet, making a loud *clack, clack, clack* sound in rapid fire. His fins are acting like kites, catching the wind and pulling him aft. Drew's head is on a swivel, trying to locate the raft below while being blown and spun by the wind. He is streaming far aft of the helicopter, so that the raft is much too far away, way out in front of him.

Drew, dangling at the end of the cable, is absolutely blown away by the size of the waves. He's glad he elected to go down by strop, because if he were on the hook, he would have to be lowered into the water, and a wave might drop out from under him before he had a chance to unhook. That would mean he'd fall to the end of the cable slack, and he'd be jerked to a stop like a rag doll. With the strop, he has more control, because all he has to do is raise his arms and he's free.

Up in the helicopter cabin, Scott is on his stomach, using all his strength to push the cable forward, to keep it away from the tail rotor, the external fuel tank, and the back end of the sliding cabin door. He's using every bit of muscle in his six-foot frame, and his voice is strained as he conns the pilots to move the aircraft forward. The helicopter lurches ahead, and now the rescue swimmer is a bit too forward of the raft. "Back twenty feet," says Scott. Aaron eases up on the power, but the winds are so strong that the Jayhawk shoots farther back. Scott shouts, "Hold, hold, hold!"

The sheer force of the wind has taken all fluidity out of the helicopter's movements, and it flies erratically. To Scott, it seems the helicopter's motions are at warp speed, and instead of calmly saying, "Back right forty, back right thirty, back right twenty," he's barking out positions in staccato style.

"Okay, forward ten feet." The helicopter lumbers forward into the wind, but the raft is drifting so fast that they've overshot it. Scott has done many hoists off moving boats, but the raft's movements are hard to time. When it is in the trough of a wave, it slows down, but when the next wave reaches it, the raft shoots forward with the wave.

"Ease back ten feet. Good, now hold! Swimmer is in position!"

Drew is within about ten feet of the wave crests but a full eighty feet from the troughs. The raft, sliding with the seas, is about thirty feet away, and he realizes Scott has gotten him as close as he can. Drew knows it's time, knows he's got to do this just right. He feels an electric jolt of energy course through his body as he watches a big roller rumble toward him. When the snarling crest passes five feet below, Drew raises his arms and plunges out of the strop.

Scott's eyes widen as he watches Drew hit the water while the cable and the strop go whipping toward the rear of the aircraft. "Oh no!" he mutters. He's retracting the cable as fast as possible, worried it will get jammed in the external fuel tank.

Even when he has the hook and strop in hand, he's concerned. *It's going to be near impossible to get either the basket or the hook back to Drew.*

Aaron has let the helicopter slide back so that he and Nevada can get a visual on Drew. Nevada is craning forward. "I can see Drew," he says. Aaron risks a brief look down and to his right, but mostly, he is sitting almost stone-still. He lightly maneuvers the cyclic and collective, focused 100 percent on keeping the Jayhawk at an even altitude and following the conning from either Nevada or Scott.

"Big wave coming," says Nevada in as calm a voice as possible.

Aaron was watching the same approaching wave, and he powers up another ten feet. The wave is a monster and rolls past, and Aaron thinks, *If we hadn't spotted that one coming, that could have been way too close.*

19

"HE NEEDS TO GO FIRST . . ."

The second Drew hit the water, he started swimming as fast as he could. Now he's trying to go even faster, afraid that he won't catch the raft before a wave breaks and buries him in its churning fury. If that happens, he'll have to start all over again by being ferried to the raft or hoisted back to the helicopter and then repositioned. Foam is coming through his snorkel, so he's barely taking a breath. He's got to get to the raft, and is already wondering if he can do this three times.

Rudy and Ben are amazed that the rescue swimmer is in the water and actually gaining on the raft. The tension they feel, being this close to rescue, is unbelievable. Then a wave slides between the raft and the swimmer, blocking their view, and they wonder if he's still making progress. When the wave rolls by, the swimmer is at the side of the raft.

Drew puts an elbow on the raft, spits out his snorkel, takes two deep breaths, then looks at the men and says, "How y'all doing today?"

Ben is so flabbergasted by what he has just seen and heard that all he can do is smile. Rudy simply says, "You guys are amazing!"

Drew is relieved to hear that comment. When he first looked at Rudy's eyes, they seemed as wide as garbage can lids, and Drew was afraid the survivor was about to panic. Now he knows the man with the gray beard is okay.

Drew nods and says, "Thank you. Is anyone hurt?"

The rescue swimmer is processing information as quickly as he can. He first notes that the raft is in bad shape, that the men do not have survival suits on, and that one of the men seems unresponsive.

Ben and Rudy point down at JP. Rudy says, "He is. Broken ribs. He needs to go first."

"All right, he's coming with me."

Drew sizes up JP. He looks half dead, barely hanging on.

~

Scott is pulling the basket bails together so he can insert the hook through their tops. The basket is a metal cage about two and a half feet wide by four feet long. On each end are floats so that the top of the basket will ride even with the ocean's surface. Survivors sit with their knees bent and involuntarily hold on to its sides with a viselike grip. Although it is designed to hold six hundred pounds, there is not enough room in it to hoist two people. In some rescues, the strop is used so that the rescue swimmer and the victim can be hoisted together, but that carries more risk for the survivor, who might slip out of the strop. And it is not an option for JP, who is unable to help in the rescue.

Working inside the cabin, Scott is facing away from the doorway. This is the first time he cannot see Drew, and he's concerned, racing to complete the task. As soon as the basket is on the hook, Scott moves back to the doorway, lies on his stomach, and waits for Drew to let him know when he is ready with the first survivor. He feels as if he is watching a science-fiction movie play out below. Few people on earth have ever seen waves this big, and it's almost inconceivable that men are in the middle of it and still alive. He can see Drew's neon-yellow helmet at the side of the raft, and he knows Drew will be hollering out the procedure for rescue to the survivors.

Come on, come on, frets Scott, *hurry up.* He's anxious to start lowering the metal cage, knowing that it might take several attempts to reposition the helicopter and get the basket close enough for Drew and the first survivor to reach it. Scott also wonders about the first survivor to be taken from the raft. *Jeez, I hope he's cooperative. Drew's never going to pull this off with a panicked and aggressive victim.*

In the cockpit, Aaron can feel the beads of sweat trickling down his chest inside his dry suit. Now that the rescue swimmer is in the water and they are waiting to lower the basket, he has climbed in altitude, to be on the safe side.

Aaron cannot see Drew or the life raft, but one thought has been bothering him for the last few minutes: *This is taking an awful long time.* He's worried the seas are overpowering the rescue swimmer and the wind will be too much for the hoist operator to perform a safe extraction of survivors. He's also reconsidering his earlier thought that they would have plenty of fuel so they could take their time with the rescues. With everything moving much more slowly than normal, Aaron is concerned they may not have time to rescue all three survivors.

As if reading his mind, Nevada says, "Scott should be lowering the basket any second. Do you need a break? Do you want me to fly?"

"I'm okay."

"You're doing great."

A gust rocks the helicopter. Nevada thinks, *Thank God for our mechanics.* He knows that all the hours of maintenance and repairs put in back at the air station make the difference between success or aborting the mission or even catastrophe. *It's going slow,* Nevada reasons, *but everyone is calm and doing their job.*

"Turn him around!" shouts Drew, referring to JP. "I want his back by the edge of the raft!"

Rudy and Ben slide the unconscious captain around and to the side of the raft. Drew puts his arms under JP's and pulls the survivor's back in tight to his own chest. He then uses his feet to push against the raft and drags JP out.

JP stirs, and his eyes flutter open. A voice in his ear says, "We're going for a basket ride."

Drew has no idea whether JP has heard him or is processing what he's saying. For now, the rescue swimmer is relieved that the injured man isn't moving. Drew has JP in what is called a cross-chest carry, with his right arm over JP's right shoulder and his hand under JP's left armpit. The maneuver allows him to tow JP a short distance from the raft.

Looking up at the helicopter, Drew gives the thumbs-up sign to indicate he is ready for the basket. He knows that Scott or the pilots have seen him, because the aircraft immediately moves forward while descending. A wave partially breaks on the men, pushing them both under, and Drew does his best to raise JP's head above the foam.

Scott slides the basket to the doorway. With his left hand, he pushes it outside the cabin while, with his right hand, he works the pendant, and the basket begins its descent. The wind blows it toward the back of the aircraft. Scott, who is now on his stomach, wrestles with the cable, pulling it forward so that the basket and cable don't get pushed into the tail rotor or the external fuel tank.

Nevada is scanning the instruments and alerting the C-130 of their progress while keeping his eye on the clock and the oncoming waves. He's growing fretful about the slow pace due to the seas. As quietly and calmly as possible, he says, "How's it going back there, Scott?"

"Basket is being lowered," gasps Scott.

From Drew's perspective, the deployment is not going well. The basket is streaming about thirty feet behind the aircraft. Drew catches a glimpse of Scott in the doorway, struggling with the 130-foot cable. The Jayhawk slowly advances past his position in the ocean, bringing the trailing basket closer. Drew is having a hard time seeing the basket because of the foam scudding along the ocean's surface like tumbleweed rolling through a desert. The downdrafts from the helicopter's rotors add to the chaos, sending a swirling froth in all directions.

Drew surges upward, using his flippers to gain a bit of height, and sees that the basket is only twenty-five feet away. He makes his move, knifing through the water with JP under one arm. Just a few feet before his objective, out of the corner of his eye, he sees a wave looming overhead. He grabs a bite of air before he and JP are pummeled by collapsing white water of such force that Drew is stunned and truly frightened. *Whatever happens, don't let go of this man,* Drew tells himself. He's not sure which way is up or down, but he tries to stay calm, knowing that the buoyancy in his dry suit, coupled with JP's PFD, will bring them to the surface. When his head clears the foam, he has swallowed a good deal of seawater, and he wonders if the limp man in his arms is still alive. Drew treads water and steals a look at JP, noting his quivering purple lips, yet he's surprised to see the survivor's eyes open.

The basket is now far away, and Drew waits, knowing Scott will vector the pilots back into position, where the cage will be closer. He watches the aircraft maneuvering for another pass, and he is determined not to miss the opportunity. When the basket is ten feet away, Drew rushes forward to grab it. This time he almost has a hand on its metal bars when the wave beneath him drops away. The rescue swimmer and the survivor go sliding down the wave's back side while the basket is airborne with no water beneath it.

Drew can't believe it. He's wasting valuable energy, and he doesn't even have the first survivor in the basket. He has no idea how much time has gone by since he entered the water, but it seems like a lot. *Ten minutes? Twenty minutes?* And getting the survivor into the basket is sometimes the hardest part, particularly if the survivor can't help in the process.

Up above, Scott is angry. He's still on his belly, straining against his safety belt, holding the cable forward with his left hand while working the hoist with his right. Because the basket is far behind the helicopter, he has to keep his eyes on that spot rather than looking ahead for oncoming waves. He is conning the pilots into a position thirty feet in front of the men in the water below, but he is also listening for Nevada to warn him of any really big waves approaching. *This is taking way too long. Wonder what the fuel situation is.* Then he stops the thought sharply. *That's the pilots' concern. Just focus on your job.*

The aircraft crew members aren't the only ones anxious about the passing time. Rudy and Ben, still in the drifting raft, are now far from the action. They can no longer see JP and the rescue swimmer, and with each passing wave, their glimpses of the helicopter are becoming briefer and briefer, until it's mostly out of sight.

Rudy is cold to the core, and he's having trouble gripping the raft's lifeline. *Something's wrong,* he thinks, *but they won't leave us. You made it this far—you can hang tough a little longer.*

20

AS IF SHOT
FROM A CANNON

Once again Scott has conned the pilots into position and manipulated the cable so that the basket is just ten feet from Drew and JP. Drew makes his move, dragging the survivor with a burst of renewed energy, knowing he has to get JP into the basket before they are carried to a wave crest. This time his free hand grabs hold of one of the metal bars surrounding the cage. He feels the seconds ticking by. The worst scenario would be if only half of JP's body is in the basket when a wave drops out from under them. The slack in the cable will instantly snap taut, and without water to support the basket, any number of injuries could befall JP, including getting his neck broken by the abrupt motion.

Drew pivots to pull JP up to the side bar of the basket and, continuing that motion, gets the semiconscious survivor's torso inside. He feels a wave lifting them up. The rescue swimmer puts one arm under JP's legs and heaves upward with all his might. He's got two-thirds of JP's body inside the basket, and he quickly picks up the survivor's dangling legs and jams them inside as well. Not wasting a moment, he holds on to the side bar with one hand and begins to use the other to give the thumbs-up signal to Scott. But as he's doing so, a jagged wave crest passes beneath them. The basket is ripped from Drew's grip, and he looks up to see JP and the basket go shooting skyward as if shot from a cannon.

Up above, Scott sees the whole episode play out, holding his breath as the basket jerks violently at the end of the cable. He curses to himself and thinks, *We're killing the survivor before we even rescue him.* The burly flight mechanic is on his knees at the open doorway, retracting the cable as fast as it will go to pull the survivor up. When the basket is at the door, Scott leans out and uses each of his hands to grab different bails. JP's back is to Scott, and he is slumped in an awkward reclining position, with his knees fully bent. It looks as if he has been stuffed into the basket and then forcibly jammed down.

Scott has no idea whether JP is dead or alive. The survivor's head is underneath a yellow inflatable PFD that has risen and, instead of being around his chest and neck, is wrapped around his face. For better traction, Scott lifts his left leg so that his foot is on the floor, and then he muscles the steel cage partway into the aircraft, giving JP a real jolt. Then Scott pulls straight back and slides the basket toward the rear of the cabin.

Suddenly, like Lazarus rising from the dead, JP lifts an arm, then struggles to sit up straight. Scott, still kneeling behind JP, grabs him under the arms and starts lifting while JP pushes with his feet, raising his butt from the bottom of the basket. Incredibly, JP arches his back so that it is on the side of the basket, and then he rolls out. The broken ribs take a real pounding, but so many of JP's senses are awakening at once that he barely feels it. His mind is slowly starting to process his surroundings. *I'm not dead. Someone is helping me.*

Scott helps the survivor toward a bench opposite the open doorway, and JP sits. Part of his ashen face is now showing above his PFD, and he looks like a zombie. His expression is dazed, and his eyes stare blankly. The noise from the helicopter is deafening, and it seems to cause JP to come out of shock. He looks around and realizes he is inside a helicopter.

As JP's brain kicks into full consciousness, his first thought is: *Where are the others? They can't be gone, they can't be dead.*

❧

In the cockpit, Aaron feels a bit of relief that one survivor is in the cabin, but now his concern is directed at Drew. Compared to the life raft, Drew is a mere speck in the ocean, a much smaller visual target. Aaron repositions the helicopter closer to Drew. The rescue swimmer is down in a trough and can barely be seen. *If we lose sight of him, we will never find him.*

Nevada hurriedly shouts, "Large wave approaching!"

Aaron quickly nudges up the power to climb out of danger. He then watches as the colossal roller sweeps up the rescue swimmer and carries him skyward. Drew is lifted so high, he is almost at the same level as Aaron. *Man, I can see his face!* thinks Aaron. The copilot is sitting stock-still; one would never know his pulse is racing. His mind is galloping ahead as well, trying to visualize the next steps. *We're going to be lucky if we can get him back . . . and even luckier if we get those remaining on the raft.*

Aaron considers asking Nevada if he thinks they can successfully hoist the swimmer back. He wants reassurance. But he says nothing, telling himself, *Now is not the time.*

Down in the cauldron, Drew is winded. His heart feels as if it is going to jump out of his dry suit. After being lifted by the big wave toward the nose of the helicopter, he's now being pushed aft of the aircraft and directly behind it. Thinking he's in a blind spot, he swims forward and out to the two o'clock position. Another wave pushes him back, this one dunking and spinning him. He surfaces quickly and looks skyward. The helicopter is gone. Just a few seconds ago, he felt as if he could reach out and grab its landing gear, and now, walled in between two waves, the swimmer can see only a small patch of empty sky overhead. He cannot hear the rotors amid the wind roaring and the waves crashing. Briefly, he thinks the helicopter might have crashed. Then he tells himself to stay positive. *You've got the best pilots up there.*

Craning his neck, Drew tries to see more sky and less wave, but he has no sight of the aircraft. He's not sure which way to swim, so he floats and tries to catch his breath. The enormity of the waves and the seriousness of his predicament fully dawn on him. *What did I get myself into?*

~

Scott is back at his perch by the cabin door. He had a brief view of Drew, but now the rescue swimmer is nowhere to be seen. "Back fifty feet," Scott commands through his headset. The flight mechanic lies down on his stomach and shimmies the upper part of his body as far out as he dares, looking beneath the aircraft. "I see the swimmer! Go back ten more feet."

JP is anxiously watching Scott. He isn't sure what's going on, but he knows it's not good. Without a headset on, he cannot hear Scott say that he saw Drew. Even though the door is open, the helicopter is warmer than the water, and JP is thinking a bit more clearly. *They can't find the swimmer or the raft.* He can feel panic rising, yet there is not a thing he can do.

"Lowering the hook for swimmer," announces Scott. *It would be nice if I could actually see the swimmer longer than a second or two.* Instead of lowering the strop, Scott is lowering the bare hook for less wind resistance.

As the helicopter finally comes into Drew's field of vision, he thinks it's the most beautiful sight he's ever seen. He's so elated, so focused on the hook coming down, that he gets blindsided by a wave breaking directly on him. He is under-water longer than the last time he was buried, and his body is screaming that it needs air. Not sure which way is up, he starts to kick with his flippers, hoping he's heading in the right direction.

About three seconds later, his head clears the surface, and he immediately sucks in a deep breath through his snorkel. He gets a mouthful of seawater and starts choking. Kicking hard with his flippers, he pushes his head above the foam and finally grabs a bite of air. He feels nauseated, spent. Being in a dry suit isn't helping matters—he feels as if he is swimming in-side it, not from seawater but from his own sweat. The water temperature is seventy degrees, but it could easily have been in the upper fifties if they were just a few miles away, outside the Gulf Stream eddy. If he can't get safely back on the helicopter, the dry suit just might save his life.

Earlier, he and Scott decided that once the first survivor was safely aboard, Drew would be "air-taxied" back to the raft instead of being hoisted into the helicopter. This would be quicker than another redeployment.

Now Drew is having second thoughts. He's thinking about the way JP shot up into the air on the basket and wonders if the strop is the way to go for the next rescue. *Maybe I should talk to Scott.* Drew is also thinking that being in the helicopter for a minute will allow him to breathe real air, not foam and mist. He needs to get his wind back, but he doesn't want to leave the men in the raft any longer than he has to. *I'll decide once I'm airborne.*

In an effort to reduce the gyrations of the cable, the pilots are keeping the helicopter low, just ninety feet above the wave trough. Still, the hook is a moving target. When the hook is ten feet away, Drew swims to it. Grabbing it is difficult; one minute it is five feet above him and out of reach, and the next it's underwater. He's leery about snatching the cable itself, worried that it might shred his hand if a wave drops out from under him. Finally, in the relative safety of a trough, he grabs hold of the hook.

Drew is wearing a body harness with straps that wrap around the waist, under the legs, up the back, and over the shoulders, then down the chest to reconnect at the waist. He quickly attaches the hook to a point on his waist and gives the thumbs-up sign, relieved to be connected to the aircraft.

Scott announces, "Swimmer is on the hook." He retracts some line so that Drew is just above the wave tops. "Swimmer is one-third up. We can air-taxi him to the raft." Scott has no idea where the raft is but assumes the pilots either can see it or will start searching downwind.

Aaron eases off the power, allowing the wind to push back the helicopter. The wind blows it too hard, making it lurch, and the copilot struggles to stabilize it and slow the speed.

Down below, Drew is skimming just over the wave tops at the end of the hoist line. He makes up his mind that he needs to talk to Scott, and he pats the top of his head, which is the signal to be brought in. Immediately, the cable starts lifting him, though the blasts of wind push Drew in long arcing swings like the pendulum of a clock, making the rescue swimmer dizzy.

Nevada's head is in constant motion. One second he's looking ahead to call out any really large waves, and the next he's watching the cabin door, eager for Drew to appear on the hook. When the swimmer is up and inside, Nevada clenches and pumps his fist with pride. He likens this rescue to a boxing match, with Drew as the fighter who has just gotten through round one. Instead of sitting in his corner of the ring, Drew is sitting on the floor, completely out of breath. He hears Scott say, "Are you okay?" Drew nods and then vomits on the cabin floor.

If Drew is the fighter, Scott is the trainer, and he's watching his man closely, making sure he is a go for the next round. "Are you sure you can do this?" he asks.

Catching his breath, Drew says to Scott, "I'll be fine. What do you think about using the strop for the next rescue?"

Scott pauses, thinking how the wave fell out from under the basket just as JP was stuffed into it. "I don't think the strop will be any different. You and the survivor could be jerked even harder on the strop. It would save time, but the more I think about it, the more I think it's too risky."

Drew nods, deferring to Scott, since the flight mechanic will be the one managing the hoist.

Nevada can hear Scott's side of the conversation, knows what they're talking about, and agrees. He turns forward and assists Aaron in searching for the raft. "How you holding up?" he asks.

"Good. But this is unreal. I don't see the raft anywhere."

"Well, it was drifting faster than I've ever seen a raft or a boat drift."

"Let's hope it's still afloat."

THEY'RE NOT COMING
FOR US

Rudy and Ben clutch the battered raft while wave after wave send it surging forward, away from where they last saw the helicopter. Ten minutes have gone by, and Rudy privately wonders if the pilots decided to return to base before the storm could cause a catastrophe. As a pilot himself, he can't blame them.

Ben has been searching the one patch of sky he can see between thundering rollers. He quietly says, "They're not coming for us."

"If they got one, they'll get all three of us." Rudy is nowhere near as confident as his answer indicates. In fact, he's thinking, *We don't even know if the rescue swimmer made it back up to the helicopter.* No sooner does he complete the thought than the helicopter zips over a wave, about a hundred yards off to the right. "They're still here!" shouts the Canadian.

The helicopter is out of sight for a moment, and then it is back, this time flying to a spot directly above the raft, where it holds in a hover.

"Okay," says Ben, "you go next."

"No, it's your turn now."

"Listen," says Ben, "I don't even feel cold, and you're shivering. You have a family—I'm single. You go next."

Rudy nods. There is no time to argue: he can see the swimmer sitting at the open doorway, feet dangling outside the aircraft, ready to be lowered.

Up in the cockpit, Aaron, well aware of how long everything is taking, speaks to Scott through his headset. "I'm going to try to help you guys by coming down in altitude to see if I can minimize your hoisting distance."

In an amazing display of control, the copilot lowers the aircraft into the trough, so the crest of the next approaching wave is higher than the helicopter. Aaron has found a rhythm. When the crest is about forty feet away, he increases altitude, lets it pass, and then lowers the helicopter back into the next trough. This simple but risky maneuver makes a world of difference for both Scott and Drew as the swimmer is lowered. Instead of Drew trailing forty feet behind the helicopter because of the wind, he is only about twenty feet aft. Scott is able to time Drew's descent into the water to coincide with the back side of a wave rather than the front, where it could break on him.

Scott manages to position Drew fifteen feet downwind from the raft. Drew releases and barely has to take a stroke; the raft is carried on a wave almost straight to him. Drew is thankful beyond words; he's dog-tired, and this allows him to conserve a little energy for the two remaining rescues, as well as the final hoist to get himself out of the watery chaos.

The swimmer puts an arm on the raft, spits out his snorkel, and asks who's next.

Ben points to Rudy.

Drew explains he will drag Rudy to the basket.

Rudy watched the procedure with JP, so he knows what to do. He turns to Ben and says that he will see him up in the plane. Then Rudy rolls out of the raft and lets Drew pull him a few feet away from the little vessel that has kept them alive against all odds. The basket is lowered within seconds, and Drew helps him inside it. Rudy now knows why two of them don't go up together; there is barely enough room for one.

Once he's in the basket, the effects of hypothermia, stress, and exhaustion sweep down on him, enveloping him in bone-crushing stiffness. Maybe it's because he is in someone else's care, or maybe it's because he's no longer watching over JP, but whatever the reason, his body feels like it weighs a ton. He can sense the basket twisting and spinning, but he pays it no mind, too tired to even lift his head and look at the helicopter above him.

Scott is waiting at the door, working the pendant. When the basket arrives, he hauls it in. He's concerned about this survivor. The gray-bearded man struggles to get out of the basket, and when he does, he lands on all fours, with seawater pouring out of his foul-weather gear. Then he collapses on the cabin deck, rolling over on his back.

Scott is thinking heart attack. "Are you okay?" he shouts.

"Yes," gasps Rudy, "I'll be all right."

While Scott goes to work freeing Rudy from the inflatable life vest, JP, who has been sitting on the bench on the opposite wall, rallies and reaches out to his friend. He holds Rudy's shoulder as if unable to believe he's safe.

Rudy struggles to sit up, then collapses back into JP and Scott. The flight mechanic has his face inches from Rudy's, checking his breathing, searching his eyes.

"I'll be okay," says Rudy. "Don't worry about me. Do your job."

Scott is thrilled to hear the survivor talking, making sense. He knows that precious seconds are ticking by. He is feeling the strain of not knowing where Drew is, as well as their fuel constraints that dictate when they must leave, which pilots call the "bingo" time.

Scott sees that Rudy cannot raise himself, and with a surge

of pure power, the flight mechanic crouches, grabs Rudy under his right arm, and pulls him up and onto the bench next to JP.

With tears in his eyes, JP embraces Rudy. Both men never expected to be alive, never dreamed a rescue was possible. Whatever pain is shooting through JP's ribs is ignored as he holds his friend and says, "You made it, you made it."

While Rudy was being hoisted, the life raft carrying the last survivor has drifted far from the scene. Ben is alone, and four long minutes have gone by without a glimpse of the helicopter. Somehow the angry ocean seems more desolate, more menacing, making Ben feel forlorn and insignificant. He tries to stay positive, but he knows a number of different scenarios might have cropped up, making his rescue impossible. Ben's immediate concern, however, is hanging on to the life raft. With the other two men gone, the raft is much lighter and is surfing down waves at terrifying speeds. He is clutching the vessel's lifeline with all the strength he has. While he can't control what is happening with the helicopter, he knows he's as good as dead if he gets separated from the raft.

Drew is more than a couple hundred yards away from Ben, and although he is not with the raft, his position is the safer of the two. The helicopter is overhead, and the pilots aren't taking their eyes off him, positioning the aircraft so that Drew is always in sight.

Scott has moved the basket to a secure location in the cabin and attached the strop to the hook. "I'm lowering the strop," he announces to the pilots. "Go forward thirty feet."

Aaron moves the helicopter forward, waits for a wave crest to pass, and then lowers the helicopter into the trough.

Drew has no trouble swimming to the strop. He positions it around his chest and under his arms, then gives the thumbs-up sign. By prearrangement with Scott, they are going to air-taxi Drew to the raft to eliminate a complete hoisting and lowering of the swimmer. Drew can always change his mind and be returned to the helicopter simply by patting his head.

Scott retracts about forty feet of cable and tells the pilots that they can begin the search for the raft. Aaron brings the helicopter up another twenty feet and lets the wind slowly blow them backward. Drew is sailing a good thirty feet behind the helicopter and feels like he's moving at warp speed.

The rescue swimmer has no idea how long the hunt for the raft will take, so he tries to relax and visualize another successful survivor hoist. But the scene just below his flippers is too riveting for him to look away. He cannot believe the size of the waves and is mesmerized by the way the wind snatches the top two feet of the crests and sends the spray and foam hurling through the air, far ahead of the roller itself. Sometimes the wind shifts a bit and peels back the top part of the wave, blowing it skyward. The waves range from fifty to seventy feet, with an occasional monster exceeding that height. One colossal wave comes so close to Drew that he feels he could sit right down on the crest, and when it passes and he is dangling above the trough, it looks like the bottom of the canyon is a mile below him.

Drew sees the raft about the same time the rest of his crew does, and he shakes his head in wonder. *It looks like a surfboard! Scott will have to get me really close.*

As soon as a wave crest passes beneath the raft, Drew can feel himself being lowered. He's not sure whether the helicopter is descending or cable is being fed out. Whatever the technique, it works, because as the raft slides down into the next valley, Drew is only fifteen feet above it and downwind about twenty feet. *This is as close as they're going to get me.* Up come his arms, and he falls from the sling feetfirst. As soon as he hits the water, he's sprinting to the raft. *I can't miss it. I've got to get it on this first try.* Like the pilots worrying about the helicopter's fuel, Drew is cognizant of his energy limits. The swimming, grappling with the basket, and ingestion of seawater are all taking a toll on the rescue swimmer. If the speeding raft gets past him, he'll have to waste precious energy getting back in the strop and being lifted once again.

A breaking sea rolls him, and when Drew emerges from the turbulence, he's not sure where the raft is. He swivels around. *There it is! It's getting by me!* He puts his head down and kicks for all he's worth, intersecting the path of the raft before it is gone.

Ben reaches out and holds on to Drew's harness. Drew, gasping for air, spits out the snorkel and holds on to the raft for a couple of seconds, gathering himself. "Okay!" he shouts to Ben. "Come out backward. But before we leave, I need to stab the raft!"

Ben gives Drew an incredulous look. Puncturing the raft means that if his hoist—or Drew's final hoist—fails, the raft will no longer be there as an emergency backup.

Despite his surprise, Ben slides from the raft and into the churning sea.

Drew pulls him in close and shouts in his ear, "I'm going to need my hands free! Grab on to my harness and hold on as tight as you can!" While he is talking, Drew feels something bump into his shoulder, and it's not Ben. The rescue swimmer is startled and spins around. Floating in the water is the malfunctioning GPIRB, which came free of its tether. Drew reaches out and grabs it, stuffing the mechanism in the pocket of his dry suit. He's not sure if it's working, but he doesn't want to chance an emergency device giving off a signal for a rescue that's already done. That line of reasoning is why he's going to sink the raft. If the raft somehow managed to stay afloat for another couple of days, it's possible that a ship would spot it and a whole new rescue might be launched.

Reaching into a pocket on his vest, Drew withdraws his knife, first stabbing the raft, then using a sweeping motion to put a big slice in it. The raft deflates, though part of it stays on the surface. Drew locks one arm around Ben and tows him a few feet away, using his free arm to motion to Scott for the basket.

Ben is the heaviest of the three survivors, and Drew is nearing total exhaustion when the basket arrives. He's relieved when Ben crawls inside the basket with little help, then alarmed when Ben crouches with his hands on the bails. Drew shouts, "Sit down and keep your knees up by your chest."

Now that the helicopter is directly overhead, Ben can't hear a word Drew is saying.

Drew tries a different approach. He motions for Ben to sit and at the same time hits the back of the survivor's knees, which forces him to go down. Ben now understands and gives Drew a thumbs-up as he is carried skyward, leaving the rescue swimmer alone in the ocean.

～

Scott uses his left arm to push the cable as far away from the aircraft as possible while it slowly retracts through his gloved hand. He suddenly stops the hoist. Frayed strands of cable have sliced through his glove, just missing his skin. With the jerking motion of the helicopter, it's hard to see how many strands have broken free. He's processing the problem as fast as he can, knowing that cutting the cable above the frayed section and reattaching a new cable will take far too long.

Scott is worried not that the frayed cable will break but that it may get balled up and stuck in the hoist. He makes a quick decision and resumes the hoist, calculating—and praying—that the cable will make both this hoist and the final one for Drew.

22

HE'S GOING TO DROWN

Against all odds, the final survivor is being hoisted to safety. Ben isn't wild about heights, and he grips the basket with all his strength, surprised by how thin the cable is that supports him. As he nears the helicopter and the deafening *thock-thock-thock* of its rotors, he fears the basket will be drawn right into the steel underside of the aircraft.

JP, sitting against the wall opposite the cabin door, is thinking clearly now, in part owing to the warmth of the cabin. He has no idea that Ben is on his way up, and he senses that something has gone wrong; several minutes have gone by since Rudy was retrieved. JP is worried sick that Ben won't make it, and he feels responsible, going back over every decision he made, second-guessing himself, cursing the GPIRB that went dead.

He's startled out of his ruminations when the basket carrying Ben is at the door.

Scott guides the basket inside, and Ben gets a leg out and rolls onto the floor. JP and Rudy reach out, tapping his head, patting his shoulder repeatedly, as if to make sure it is really Ben, not a hallucination. Ben sits facing his friends and gives them a quick thumbs-up, a surprised look on his face, not quite believing he is out of the raft and up in the sky.

~

Roller after giant roller slides under the rescue swimmer, who is vomiting violently, his body trying to rid itself of the seawater he has ingested. Drew faces the awful truth that all his laps in the pool, weight lifting, ocean simulated rescues, and various other forms of training are no match for waves of this magnitude. He has been exerting himself nonstop for almost half an hour, and he's spent. Over and over he tells himself, *Just hang on for a couple more minutes.* But time has lost its normal progression, and seconds feel like minutes, minutes like hours.

Then disaster. A giant wave breaks directly on the swimmer, driving him down while he has his mouth open in the act of vomiting. He can feel himself ingesting more seawater, coughing and choking as he tumbles inside the maw of the wave. He claws at the water, trying to propel his body in the direction he thinks is the surface. *Air, air,* his brain screams.

Prior to this comber, Aaron and Nevada were making sure

they never lost sight of Drew, alarmed by the beating the rescue swimmer was taking. During the rescues, Drew was mostly on the surface, riding the waves like a kid on a roller coaster. But the two pilots noticed that once the rescues were complete, their swimmer was disappearing underwater every time a wave broke anywhere near him. And it seemed that when he popped back up, he barely had time to grab a breath before foam engulfed him.

Now Aaron is thinking, *This is bad. He's going to drown right in front of us.* He then watches in horror as the house-sized wave avalanches on the swimmer. White water swirls in all directions. There is no sign of Drew.

Aaron holds his breath, craning forward to spot Drew's neon-yellow helmet. *Come on, come on,* a desperate Aaron urges, *you can do it,* trying to will his swimmer to the surface.

Drew breaks through the churning water. He gulps in a mix of foam and air, frantically waving his arm back and forth over his head, the emergency signal. He's got nothing left; he needs to get out of the water, knowing he won't survive another wave like that.

Aaron sees Drew first. "I'm getting the emergency signal!" shouts the copilot. "I'm moving closer."

Scott, who is disconnecting the basket from the hook, can't believe his ears. In all his many rescues, this has never happened, and Drew is the toughest swimmer he's ever worked with. Adrenaline surges into every muscle of the flight mechanic's body, and he tells himself, *Stay calm, no mistakes.*

Technically, the rule is to lower the basket if a swimmer is in trouble. But Scott decides against it, thinking that Drew might have cramped up and may not be able to climb inside. And the basket, being much larger than the bare hook, will be blown far aft by the eighty-knot winds and will take longer to position close to Drew.

Scott has forgotten all about the frayed strands of the cable and starts lowering the hook, conning the pilots into the correct position to get as close as possible to Drew. Once again the flight mechanic is on his stomach, his head and shoulders outside the aircraft. The wind continues to make it hard for him to get a decent breath of air. Whenever he needs to tell the pilots anything, he has to turn his head to the side, away from the cold blasts.

Scott considers different scenarios if Drew can't get himself attached to the hook. He could try the strop but knows that will waste more time because of the way it will sail in the wind. Another option, and not a good one, is to lower the basket and try to scoop Drew up. If Drew becomes unconscious, the success of this maneuver is unlikely. But if these options don't work, there are no more. The swimmer will die.

~

Drew is treading water, watching the hook descend, hoping he won't have to swim more than a couple of strokes to it, not knowing for sure what his body is capable of at this point. With relief, he sees how Scott and the pilots have worked the helicopter so that the hook is within five feet, and he manages a couple kicks of his flippers, grabbing the hook with his right hand. He attaches it to the ring in the front of his harness located near the bottom of his rib cage. Then he notices that the harness leg straps are high up around his butt rather than around his middle thigh. *I've got to move these down. . . . If a wave falls out from under me, I'm going to take the brunt of it on my back.*

A second or two later, as Drew struggles with the straps, a wave crest passes beneath him. There is almost no slack in the cable, so he doesn't slide down the back of the wave. Instead, without the water to support his body, he is yanked so violently that his head and back jerk backward and he feels as if he has been snapped in two.

A sharp, white-hot pain shoots up Drew's back, and he moans in agony. The cable is bringing him higher, but instead of coming up in a sitting position, he has his belly at the highest point and his back arched in an awkward position. He flails his arms, trying to grab the front of his harness or the hook, anything to sit up before his back breaks.

~

Scott saw that the wave crest was catching Drew unaware, and the flight mechanic paid out cable as fast as he could. But not fast enough. He watched in horror as Drew was jerked so suddenly that his back bent like a gymnast's and his head almost touched his flippers. The helicopter actually shuddered from the weight of Drew's fall.

"Oh no!" cries Scott. Then a five-second pause. "I might have broken his back."

Aaron hears this comment through his headset, and a cold chill races up his spine. *Did I just hear that right?* He glances at Nevada, whose face is ashen. Nevada starts to say something to Scott, then thinks better of it. The pilots can't stand the tension, feel like jumping out of their skin, because there is nothing they can do. It's all up to Scott and Drew. Adding to their stress is the fact that Drew is directly below the aircraft, and neither pilot can see him.

~

Scott's right hand is pressing the pendant while the retracting cable slides through his gloved left hand. He can feel where the frayed cable strands are sticking out, and he's holding his breath, hoping the hoist mechanism doesn't jam when the loose ends are pulled through. None of this is in the script; Scott feels like everything is going all wrong and they are on the verge of disaster. The lift seems to be happening in slow motion. Scott is trying to see Drew's face, wondering if he is conscious. A million thoughts race through Scott's mind, but the dominant one is: *If his back is broken, I'll never forgive myself.*

Scott gets the swimmer to the door and hauls him in. Drew

collapses on the floor. Scott shouts, "Are you okay? Are you okay?"

Drew can't talk but tries to nod. He's having trouble breathing, and his back is spasming. He looks up and sees the three survivors staring at him, and his training starts to kick in. As the aircraft's emergency medical technician, he has to look after the survivors, and he knows one of them has broken ribs. He strains to sit up.

"Drew!" shouts Scott. "Lie back down!"

"I'm fine."

"No, you're not fine. I saw what happened. Let me get you a neck brace."

Drew somehow manages to sit up and slides toward JP. He puts an oxygen mask on the injured survivor. He leans toward JP and shouts in his ear, "Are you okay?" Then he checks on the other two survivors.

The pilots are blasting the heat, but Drew is chilled. There is a considerable amount of water inside his dry suit—both sweat and ocean—and it's making him shiver. He's lightheaded and woozy and moves toward the closed cabin door. He takes a sip of water and immediately feels nauseated and knows he's going to be sick again. He can feel the bile rising, and not wanting to stink up the cabin, he grabs one of his flippers and vomits into it. Then he opens a six-inch hatch in the cabin door and dumps the contents. When he turns around, the survivors are staring at him again, and Scott is shaking his head. Drew manages a weak smile and then tries to lie down, but the contractions in his back make straightening out impossible, so he sits facing the survivors, wondering if he's going to pass out.

Scott moves over to Drew and starts apologizing for not being able to let out enough cable. Drew stops him in midsentence. "Listen," says the rescue swimmer, "you got me out. That's all that matters."

CHERRY POINT NAVAL
HOSPITAL

It's hard for those of us in a comfortable setting to fully understand the psychological trauma that has enveloped Ben, Rudy, and JP. First there was the nerve-racking buildup of the waves battering the boat, hitting so hard that they boomed upon impact. That was followed by the first capsizing, which sent the men ricocheting through the cabin and colliding with one another. Then the GPIRB failed, followed by the second capsizing, after which the boat did not immediately right itself. This was when JP, with broken ribs, swam out of the boat, found the life raft pinned by the spreader, and managed to free it, cracking more ribs in the effort. Next came the boarding of the raft and the terrifying ride down massive waves that sometimes pitched the shell-shocked men into the sea. They lived through a nightmare few have endured, and the surreal experience has left them numb.

Now, flying toward land, each of the three sailors is lost in his thoughts. They don't feel like talking, but even if they did, they couldn't be heard over the whine of the engine and the roar of the rotors. JP is in pain, shivering, and exhausted. The turbulence isn't helping his ribs, and the sleep-deprived captain just wants to be on dry land. He is claustrophobic inside the helicopter, which reminds him of being inside a submarine and how, when the hatch closed, he felt entombed. He wonders how he will break the news to his wife. It's too much to think about. He steels himself for the hour-and-forty-five-minute ride back to the U.S.

His one diversion during the flight is staring at copilot Aaron Nelson, who has barely moved. Even during the rescues of Ben and Rudy, JP noticed that Aaron used the subtlest of touches to deftly make the helicopter move left or right or change altitude. He wonders how in the world the copilot has kept such focus and concentration for so long.

His beloved *Sean Seamour II* is at the bottom of the ocean, but JP is riding a wave of relief from seeing Rudy and Ben rescued. He mistakenly thought the swimmer was too exhausted to do any more after his own rescue, and he'd begun to panic at the thought that his two crewmates would be left in the storm.

~

Nevada is so proud of his crew that he needs a moment before he says anything. He composes himself and gets on the radio to the C-130 escorting them back, giving them a complete update, knowing their concern about Drew's welfare. He tells Commander Beavis in the C-130 that he marked the position when they got on scene and did the same when they picked up Drew. "We moved one point eight miles in twenty-eight minutes. That's how fast the raft was moving."

Aaron, who may look to JP like a programmed robot, is anything but. He is roasting in his dry suit. During the rescue, he had as much adrenaline coursing through his body as Drew and Scott did, but no way to burn it off. Now the heavy, sick feeling that often follows a burst of adrenaline is setting in, and he begins to feel nauseated. "Take the controls," he says to Nevada. "I'm not doing well."

Once Nevada takes over, Aaron slumps in his seat. His head hangs, and he tries not to throw up. He opens a little round air scoop in the lower portion of the Plexiglas window and bends all the way forward, letting the fresh air blow on his face, hoping for the nausea to pass. When it doesn't, he starts looking for something to vomit in and eyes the helmet bag by his seat. The whole time he's thinking, *How hot do these survivors have to be?*

~

Rather than fly back to Elizabeth City, Nevada has decided to save time by going to Marine Corps Air Station Cherry

Point. When they are within seventy-five miles of land, the C-130 peels off and heads back out to sea to search for another ship in distress. Aaron starts to wonder if he and his crew, too, will be sent back out.

Then Aaron remembers the frayed cable and realizes they would have to fly to Elizabeth City to get it replaced and pick up a new rescue swimmer.

Nevada shuts the engines down and tells the crew what a great job they did.

Cherry Point has been alerted to the injuries aboard the helicopter, and when they land, three ambulances race up to the aircraft as the pilots power it down.

Scott opens the cabin door and tells Ben, who is closest to the opening, to exit first. Emergency Medical Technicians (EMTs) escort him to an ambulance, despite his protests that he is fine.

Rudy, who has been shivering from exposure, is next. He, too, says he doesn't need to go to the hospital. But when he steps out of the helicopter, he has trouble standing. Paramedics move in and support him, then hustle him into the ambulance, where they strip off his wet clothes and wrap him in blankets with heat packs pressed against his body. They take his temperature, and it is 95 degrees—not life-threatening but still low, considering he was in the helicopter for over an hour and a half with the heater blasting.

JP comes out next, and the paramedics get him on a special board for neck and back injuries. His core temperature is about the same as Rudy's, and the medics put hot pads against his skin and cover him in blankets.

Scott helps Drew to the doorway. The paramedics place him on the special board and hustle him into one of the ambulances, where they cut off his dry suit. As they hook Drew up to an IV, Scott pokes his head inside the ambulance and pats his friend on the shoulder, still feeling that the last hoist might have ended Drew's career.

~

Rudy, Ben, JP, and Drew are all in separate rooms at the Cherry Point naval hospital. Rudy is being treated on a machine for hypothermia while his clothing is washed and dried and his passport and wallet are spread out to dry. His back aches, but the pain is manageable. Ben is feeling fine, but he's wondering how in the world he will get home to England. He didn't think to grab his passport and wallet when the boat was sinking—he didn't expect he'd be alive to use them—and now he feels a bit like he doesn't exist, as if he's in a bizarre dream.

JP, surprisingly, refuses X-rays on his broken ribs, fearing they'll mean an overnight stay in the hospital. (Later, X-rays show that ten of his ribs are broken.) Instead, he accepts a strong painkiller. Between the medication and the relief that his crew members are okay, he feels high, even a bit strong.

Drew's back is being X-rayed for possible cracked vertebrae;

fortunately, his injury is strained muscles rather than a broken back. Doctors ask if he needs morphine, and the swimmer declines but does take strong painkillers. He then rests in bed with the curtains drawn until a nurse tells him that his wife is on the phone. He is surprised that she tracked him down so quickly, and even more startled by the emotion that wells up in him when he hears her voice. Tears roll down his face, and for a moment he is unable to talk.

Later, he gets out of bed. He shuffles over to the nurses' station, where a nurse asks how his back is feeling. Drew answers, "It's better, and I'm finally starting to warm up."

"Well," says the nurse, "those other guys are starting to warm up, too."

"What other guys?"

"The three who came off the helicopter with you."

Drew is taken aback. He had no idea the survivors are at the same hospital. "You're kidding!" he exclaims. "Can I go see them?"

"Sure, they're all together in one room, having something to eat."

When Drew enters the room, he sees the three men sitting in chairs with a space heater blasting.

"Pull up a chair," says Ben.

Over the next hour, the survivors tell Drew what happened to them on the sailboat and in the raft prior to his arrival. They explain the knockdown, how JP broke his ribs, the length of time they spent in the upside-down boat, the way they abandoned ship, and finally, their time in and out of the life raft, with no hope that help was coming.

As Drew listens, he reflects that what he went through was minor compared with this story. He hangs on every word; usually, once the survivors leave the helicopter, he never sees them again. The swimmer is awed by what these three men endured but also by their even-keeled spirit.

~

Nevada, Aaron, and Scott have flown back to Elizabeth City, where the media are waiting for them. Scott and Aaron duck out and leave Nevada alone to answer questions. When he's finished, he walks into the Operations Center and describes the mission, and other pilots think he's exaggerating about the waves. "Ask Drew, Scott, and Aaron—they'll confirm it. Aaron and I both saw the altimeter swing more than seventy feet. We got some video we can show you later."

Scott knows another crew will use the helicopter to look for the *Flying Colours*, so the first thing he does is alert the mechanics in Maintenance Control to the frayed strands on the cable. A mechanic gets to work but soon walks over to Scott and says, "I checked the cable, and it's fine."

"How far did you run it out?"

"Fifty feet."

"Run it out a hundred feet."

The mechanic looks at Scott like he's lost his mind. Hoists are normally done within fifty feet of the water. But this wasn't a normal mission. With waves topping seventy feet, the helicopter was usually at an altitude of ninety to a hundred feet to avoid being taken out by a wave.

Sure enough, after the mechanic extracts a hundred feet of cable, the frayed strands are clearly visible. The entire cable is replaced.

Next Scott walks over to the C-130 crew and shakes their hands, saying a simple thank-you. Then he heads home. He doesn't feel elated but keeps replaying over and over how he let Drew fall off the wave.

~

Aaron heads straight home after taking off his gear, still feeling ill. His wife, who doesn't know about the extreme conditions he flew into, remarks that he is home earlier than she expected.

Aaron nods. He feels like he has been gone for a week. He then lies down on the living room floor.

She asks what's the matter.

Aaron doesn't know where to start. He massages his temples. Then he explains the giant seas, the hurricane-force winds, and the three men in the raft. When he describes what happened to Drew and how worried he was that they wouldn't get him back in the helicopter, he chokes up, surprised by the emotion pouring out.

At the end of the story, images of what happened keep flickering through his mind. Then he falls into a deep sleep.

24

HEADING HOME

JP's stepmother can finally rest easy. Geoff Pagels at SAR Headquarters continually updated her and let her know that all three sailors on the *Sean Seamour II* were rescued. Later, JP calls Betty and says he's okay, electing not to tell her about the broken ribs or how lucky he is to be alive.

"Can I call Mayke?" Betty asked.

"Yes. I can't call overseas from here. Just tell her I'm okay and not to worry."

Betty immediately dials Mayke in France, but when she picks up the phone, Betty hesitates, not sure how to begin.

"Hi, Mayke, it's Betty. How are you?

Mayke, who had the vision of the boat in trouble, quickly asks, "What's the matter?"

Betty pauses. "Are you sitting down?" She hears Mayke take a deep breath. Betty plows ahead. "Listen, JP is fine. But the boat is gone. There was a terrible storm."

"I knew it, I knew it!" cries Mayke. "I had those terrible dreams."

The two women talk a while longer, with Betty passing along what she learned from Geoff Pagels and JP.

After Mayke hangs up, she stares out the window. She is relieved that her husband is physically okay, but she feels ill over the loss of the boat and the impact of the ordeal on JP. He spent countless hours working on the vessel, improving it in a myriad of ways, and he had many personal items on board. She knows its loss will be a bitter blow, but she's more concerned about what happened to her husband in the storm, what trauma he will try to hide from her.

~

The three survivors are released from the hospital and given spending money from the Red Cross: enough for food, lodging, and transportation on their trek back into the land-based world. While the clothes the men had on in the water—pants and shirts—are being cleaned, they head to the PX, the store for servicemen and servicewomen at Cherry Point.

JP purchases a pair of shoes and decides to keep the box to use as his "luggage," thinking how, in twenty-four hours, he has gone from captain of a beautiful vessel to captain of a shoe box. He still can't get his head around what happened; his emotions bounce between numbness and a sensation that the last two days didn't really happen and he will wake up from the nightmare. *How can it be that a storm of this magnitude wasn't forecast well in advance? And how can it be that a new GPIRB, which was just professionally recertified, died after an hour and a half?* He wants to replay everything that happened, but he is so sleep-deprived that he decides now is not the time—he just wants to make it through the rest of the day.

After getting dressed, they're driven to a Days Inn, and the man behind the counter asks if they have luggage. JP points to his shoe box. Later, the three men walk across the street from the hotel and enter a restaurant. As they are ushered to a table by a waitress, all three men look up at a television mounted on the wall. A news reporter is explaining that there's a major storm offshore and the Coast Guard rescued three sailors. The reporter says that the survivors were found in a damaged life raft being battered by eighty-foot seas.

"Those are some lucky guys," says the waitress. "I wonder what kind of shape they're in."

"Well, those guys are us," says Ben.

The waitress's jaw drops. She stares at the men, then stammers, "You're—you're serious, aren't you?"

Rudy nods.

"Well," says the waitress, "drinks are on the house."

As they listen to the broadcast, JP hears the reporter referring to a vessel named the *Lou Pantai*. *Why are they calling the Sean Seamour II by the name of my old boat, and how do they even know its name?* Again, he wants to think it through, but he's too tired to tackle the puzzle.

Over dinner, the three men discuss how they will get home. They won't be able to take a plane because neither Ben nor JP has identification. Rudy has his driver's license, so they decide to rent a car and drive to Washington, D.C., where Ben hopes to get help at the British embassy and JP at the French embassy. Having been a consultant to the French government, JP knows he is registered and is confident that he can get the paperwork for his trip back to France and Mayke.

The next morning, they rent a van rather than a car so they can stretch out. They are still exhausted, and each man needs his space as they all come to grips with what has happened. As they begin the long drive, they hear on the radio that after twenty-four hours of searching, the *Flying Colours* crew has not been found. The announcer explains that the Coast Guard has mounted a massive search by air and water, that the storm has abated, and that searchers are hopeful they will find the crew with better visibility.

The three men in the van are pessimistic. Only they know what it was like to be in the water and in a raft for hours in punishing waves. They surmise that if the crew hasn't been rescued by now, the missing sailors either will be found dead or went down with the boat. It causes the three survivors great anguish to even think about others being in the same predicament. Already someone has said to Rudy, "God saved you," and Rudy thinks, *We were just lucky. God certainly didn't choose us over the four young people on the* Flying Colours.

As they drive north, approaching Elizabeth City, they decide to call the air station and arrange to personally thank the pilots and the hoist operator who saved their lives. They learn that the men are not on duty, so they push on, resolving to write to the rescuers when they get home.

When they near Annapolis, the terrible throbbing in JP's chest worsens. Rudy, who is driving, is having back spasms that make him miserable. They stop at the first hotel they see and spend the night.

The next morning, they arrive in Washington, D.C., and after long waits at the embassies, Ben and JP receive the necessary paperwork to get home. Both men are relieved—at least they have something to prove they exist, that they are not illegal aliens or terrorists. And JP has his first new item to put in the shoe box.

They continue driving north, staying overnight in Newark, New Jersey, before taking Ben to JFK International Airport, where he says good-bye. They talk about sailing, and JP promises a cruise in the Mediterranean, but Ben wonders if he will ever see his friends again. He is numb from the ordeal, wondering about all the many twists and turns that either caused the calamity or helped them survive.

As the plane takes off, Ben stares out into the ocean. *What would have happened if I hadn't just bought that knife we used to cut the raft free of the boat? What about JP finding the strength to swim out of the overturned boat and free the raft from the mast? What if Rudy hadn't grabbed some flares as the boat was going down? What if . . .* Then he stops. There are just too many what-ifs. The things that kept them alive were the result of good decisions, luck, and maybe fate.

~

Rudy and JP drive directly to Betty's house on Cape Cod. Betty notices how quiet the two men are and how reluctant they are to talk about what they've been through. It's obvious to her that JP is in a lot of pain, but he's also got a faraway look in his eyes. She knows he's reliving what happened, going over every step. He asks her what the Coast Guard said when they first called her, and she explains they asked if she knew whether the sailboat *Lou Pantai* was out at sea.

Then it hits JP. It was the old EPIRB, the one that was swept clear of the boat during the first knockdown, that saved their lives. His mind is spinning. *What about the signal from the new GPIRB? Its light showed that it was on for an hour and a half before it died.* This marks the beginning of JP's quest to find out what really happened.

The next morning, Rudy says he will begin his drive to Ottawa. Both Betty and JP try to convince him to rest another night, but Rudy wants to be moving.

JP walks Rudy to the van. Each saved the other man's life several times in those desperate hours in the capsized boat and tattered life raft. Now they are at a loss for words. They simply embrace, then say good-bye, knowing they will have to deal with the aftermath of the experience in their own way.

~

One simple but crucial fact that everyone involved—both rescuers and survivors—can look back on with pride is how they performed under incredible stress. The three survivors, who had known each other for only a few days, worked as a team, with each man contributing in different ways to their survival. They never once argued, but instead handled the ordeal one minute at a time, each man helping the others. Even when they thought rescue would never come, something made them battle on. Just as remarkable, they never let their fear overwhelm them and turn into panic; instead, they handled themselves with dignity. The same can be said of the rescuers. This mission was fraught with so many challenges—it's truly amazing that each man focused on his job and kept making the right decisions time and time again. All it would have taken is one wrong decision, one moment of panic, and the outcome could have been different.

Each man simply did his best and never gave up trying to do the right thing, and together they accomplished what appeared to be impossible.

EPILOGUE

Jean Pierre (JP) de Lutz

The two years after the accident were difficult ones for JP. He was suffering from sleepless nights and some anxious days. He had left the business world to restore a fourteenth-century home and gardens in the South of France, yet he wasn't feeling the joy he expected while working on his hilltop home.

His wife, Mayke, knew JP was hurting and suggested he work out his problems with a therapist. Rudy, who was in frequent contact with JP, encouraged him to seek healing for post-traumatic stress disorder (PTSD). Finally, two years after the accident, he decided to try counseling.

JP describes the next months as follows:

The therapy eventually allowed me to reclaim my natural behavior and come to terms with the accident. I began to make positive changes in both perspective and priorities. First and foremost, I no longer wear a watch. Time is too precious to count it. So now I live in my time and a new-found patience. Encountering death for the second time, staring you in the eye, to be reconciled that it is your time to go, has made me appreciate the little moments in life. Every day I still learn that most of the things that upset us are not worth the aggravation. I learn to let them go or ignore them.

The last few years of my life have been the very best: to learn to appreciate the love I share with Mayke and our moments together.

RUDY SNEL

It takes a certain kind of person to cross the Atlantic Ocean in a forty-four-foot sailboat with two strangers. Most of us would not do it, even if well paid. Rudy, however, wasn't going to sit idly through his retirement before the ill-fated trip on the *Sean Seamour II*; nor has he become a couch potato after it. He continues to travel and try new adventures, and perhaps one day he will complete the transatlantic crossing.

After the accident, Rudy traveled back to Elizabeth City and visited with the helicopter crew who saved his life. In Washington, D.C., he recounted his survival story in a presentation to the Coast Guard. His goal was to share what he had learned so that others might avoid such an ordeal, and to give thanks for all those people behind the scenes who helped with his rescue. Since then, thanks to JP's efforts, the NOAA has tightened the registration procedure for EPIRBs, which may save other sailors from the hazard of duplicate serial numbers.

Rudy has become good friends with Drew Dazzo and Scott Higgins, visiting them and staying in touch. When Drew was awarded the Star of Courage by the Canadian government, both he and Scott, as well as Nevada Smith, stayed at Rudy's Ottawa home and enjoyed Canadian hospitality.

Rudy reflects on his survival at sea with humility and gratitude, expressed in the following paragraph:

Counseling for PTSD has helped explain some of the aftermath. I was able to deal with our situation calmly and rationally because, according to the psychiatrist, I was in a dissociative state (emotionally detached). Currently, even though the experience has made me more appreciative of life's moments, trivial things can be very irritating. Life will never be quite the same. My desire to sail across the Atlantic is still there. The days of sailing with JP and Ben before the storm were great! There was a relaxing sense of freedom, despite being confined to a forty-four-foot boat.

DREW DAZZO (RESCUE SWIMMER)

Drew Dazzo received the Canadian Star of Courage for saving the life of Rudy Snel. Drew is only the third American recipient of the award, which is similar to the American Medal of Honor. He is still a rescue swimmer, saving lives.

Scott Higgins (Flight Mechanic)

Scott is now serving from Cape Cod Air Station. Even on training missions, he seems to be involved in SARs. In August 2011, he was on a nighttime gunnery training mission when he and the Jayhawk helicopter crew he was flying with saw a private plane take off and then crash into the woods and erupt in a ball of fire. The crew was able to put the helicopter down about two hundred feet from the crash site. Higgins ran to the plane and found a woman in critical condition. Emergency workers from the airport arrived and decided that carrying the woman out on foot might further injure her. The Coast Guard helicopter crew returned to their aircraft and did a basket hoist to get her out of the woods and then transferred her to an air ambulance flight.

Nevada Smith (Helicopter Pilot)

Nevada and Rudy have stayed in touch since the rescue and have had two visits. Rudy came to Elizabeth City to see the USCG awards ceremony in December 2008, and Nevada went to Ottawa for Drew's Star of Courage ceremony in February 2010. Nevada has had many SAR cases during his "duty standing" years between 1995 and 2008. He considers the May 7 rescues equal to the three sorties he flew over New Orleans, in which he rescued more than 130 victims after Hurricane Katrina.

In the spring of 2010, Nevada commissioned an artist to paint *Star of Courage*, which depicts Drew surrounded by the mountainous waves as Rudy is hoisted to the helicopter. Scott is seen leaning out of the helicopter while Ben remains in the raft, awaiting his turn in the basket. The C-130 is in the background, keeping a vigilant watch. The painting is on the largest canvas that the artist, Kris Stoll, had access to in Chesapeake, Virginia. Stoll worked on it for more than six months. The painting has been popular at Coast Guard gatherings. Each of the survivors and rescuers has received a print. Having a painting done of a rescue had been on Nevada's bucket list since he was a kid. Back then, he used to ride his bike to a Ben Franklin store in Morrisonville, Illinois, and admire the pictures on the boxes of plastic model airplanes depicting fighters and bombers in dramatic scenes. He always thought, *Someday I'll be in a painting like that.*

In early 2012, Nevada received orders to be the air operations officer at Sector Columbia River in Oregon.

AARON NELSON (COPILOT)
Aaron was able to meet Rudy in 2007:

One thing I remember is he thanked me repeatedly for participating in his rescue. At the time, I couldn't completely comprehend his vantage point—after all, I was just doing my job. In early 2011, I was diagnosed with a primary brain tumor. The initial prognosis wasn't that great, but I did get lucky—I had the great fortune of being treated by Dr. Allan Friedman at Duke University Hospital in Durham. I think of

Dr. Friedman as a true "angel among us," and I can't possibly thank him enough! Perhaps now I can more closely relate to the feelings of Rudy and the rest of the crew. It's easy to think of the helicopter crew—or doctor, in my case—as the hero. But it's also important to recognize that it's a team effort. Without the Coast Guard team, the end result could have been much different on this SAR case. I'm just glad I was able to help them out, and I'm happy they're all doing well. I wish them the best in life. I may someday return to flying (crossed fingers), but for now the Coast Guard is moving me to the District 9 Command Center in Cleveland, Ohio, where I'll coordinate search and rescue efforts on the Great Lakes. To Rudy, Ben, and JP, Godspeed.

No trace of the *Flying Colours* was ever found.

~

Video of the rescue of Rudy, Ben, and JP can be found online on YouTube, "A Storm Too Soon."

AUTHOR'S NOTE AND ACKNOWLEDGMENTS

This book all started with a photo. I had seen an amazing photograph culled from the video shot by Nevada Smith that showed JP's life raft in a eighty-foot wave. My curiosity was piqued: Did the people in the raft survive? And if so, how in the world were they rescued? I wasn't planning to write a book, but Nevada changed that.

Nevada and I corresponded by e-mail and then by phone. As he recounted the rescue of the crew from the *Sean Seamour II* and shared more images with me, I became more and more interested, knowing this story had all the twists and turns I enjoy investigating. Best of all, Nevada was as patient as he was intelligent, answering my many questions, painting a vivid picture of the rescue and the people involved. And so my first thank-you is to Nevada—he was the perfect partner to get me started when I contacted him in July 2007, and he was still helping me when I completed the writing five years later.

Having Nevada in my corner was a good start, but the next

step was critical. Would the survivors want to talk about such a traumatic experience? The first name I was given was Rudy Snel's, and when I contacted him, he was a true gentleman. I knew we would work well together. It wasn't easy for him to dive back into the storm and relive those terrible hours, but he thought the story needed to be told, and he felt other mariners' lives might someday be saved by the lessons learned from his accident. One of my fondest memories from the project is the evening when Rudy and the flight mechanic, Scott Higgins, came to my house after they had been out fishing on the ocean. The three of us sat down around my porch table, and Rudy described what happened on the sailboat before the helicopter crew located the raft. Neither Scott nor I had heard all the various details of the courageous acts performed by JP, and for an hour I just let my tape recorder run while Scott and I sat mesmerized.

While researching the book, I found ten turning points where the outcome could have been disastrous if an event had not gone exactly as it had, or had happened just a second or two later. An example is when Rudy tried to shoot a flare from the raft. Out of three flares, the first two were duds, and the wind blew the third and final flare sideways into a wave. C-130 crewman Marcus Jones told me that he saw that flare only for a split second, and if it hadn't been seen, he's not sure they would have found the raft.

I contacted Ben after Rudy, and we had a good talk on Skype, as he was working in Bahrain. We never had an opportunity to meet, but he answered my questions via e-mail during the writing process. Ben once told me that he tries not to think too much about the accident because he doesn't want it to define him, and I did my best to respect that and limit my questions and probing. Ben, thank you for your time on a book that you were never pushing for.

Because the *Sean Seamour II* was JP's boat, and because of his tumultuous childhood, he bore the brunt of my detective work. But JP made my job so much easier by graciously sending me a manuscript he was writing about his life. This helped get me up to speed before we started communicating in earnest. Then JP invited me to visit him in France to continue our discussions. I asked my daughter Kristin to join me and help with the research and also to extend our trip into Italy. She jumped at the chance. Because of her partnership—as well as JP and Mayke's hospitality—I had the trip of a lifetime. During our visit, I observed just how resourceful JP is as I viewed his handiwork restoring his fourteenth-century stone home. He and Mayke have carved out a wonderful life. It was a pleasure to know that after all the turmoil in JP's earlier years, he has now found peace.

A year after that trip, JP came to New England to help his stepmother, Betty, and he stayed with me a couple of days. I remember showing JP around my home and apologizing for the clutter, saying someday soon I would break myself of my pack rat ways. JP responded, "Being a pack rat saved my life," meaning that if he hadn't kept the old EPIRB on the *Sean*

Seamour II, he wouldn't be alive today. The highlight of the visit was when Rudy came down from Canada and the three of us had dinner. The book was well on its way, and we cleared up a couple of loose ends. I was surprised that the two men's memories were in perfect sync, and glad to see that they had not lost their sense of humor because of the post-traumatic stress they endured. They were both able to talk about the accident much more openly than when I had first approached them.

This is my second book about survival during a storm in the Gulf Stream, and it prompted me to consider the stories we hear about the Bermuda Triangle. Some who believe that something mysterious is going on in the Bermuda Triangle have expanded its area all the way up to New Jersey. They ask why some boats and aircraft have disappeared without a trace, and they attribute it to paranormal or extraterrestrial influence. But for the real reason, they should look no farther than the Gulf Stream. Its warm waters can create its own microclimate, especially when there are downdrafts of cold air, causing hazards for low-flying aircraft. Boats large and small face another hazard in or near the Gulf Stream when storms funneling winds out of a northerly direction create waves that run counter to the current. As Gulf Stream experts Dane and Jenifer Clark point out, this can lead to the dreaded rogue wave. We have seen time and again how these waves can surprise a crew and swallow a boat whole, sending it to the bottom of the sea in a matter of seconds or minutes. This might explain why some vessels in the so-called Bermuda Triangle vanish with no

Mayday, while vessels in other areas, hit by the same storm, ride it out in fine shape. And as JP learned, your boat doesn't have to be in the Stream to be impacted. Its warm-water eddies, reaching out like fat tentacles, can also ensnare a boat in extreme waves.

There were many people who assisted me in this project, and I want to thank those I have yet to mention, in no particular order. From the Coast Guard, I'd like to acknowledge Jeremy Davis, Jason Trichler, Steven Banks, Brian Avelsgard, Charles Fosse, Dan Molthen, Andy Clayton, Mike Ackermann, Dan Cancetty, David McBride, Geoff Pagels, Ed Ahlstrand, Stacy Sorenson, Marcus Jones, Paul Beavis, Casey Green, Ryan Cantu, Tasha Hood, Scott Walden, Justin Cimbak, Drew Dazzo, Steve Fischer, Bill Coty, Doug Atkins, and Roberto Torres. And a big thank-you to the behind-the-scenes Coasties who provided support for the rescuers.

Outside the Coast Guard, a myriad of people inspired or helped me, and they include Betty de Lutz, Ron Burd, Mayke Sassen, Robin Lee Graham, Jenifer and Dane Clark, Peter Reich, Andy Reeve, Mary Grinavic, Diana Rogers, Carol Dale, Michael Borisoff, Steven Callahan, John Clayman, and Luke Wiedman (future rescue swimmer!).

Other writers whose work helped in my research include Doug Campbell at *Soundings* magazine, who first wrote about the storm; William MacLeish, who wrote about the Gulf Stream; Robin Lee Graham, who wrote about his solo voyage; and the USCG Historian's Office.

Christy Ottaviano, my editor at Henry Holt, is a real pro, helping to guide me in crafting this book. Her suggestions made *A Storm Too Soon* a better book.

I'd also like to thank the readers who have shared kind words and come to my presentations. Those gestures give me energy.

ABOUT THE AUTHOR

MICHAEL J. TOUGIAS is the author of many true rescue stories, including *The Finest Hours: The True Story of a Heroic Sea Rescue*; *Fatal Forecast: An Incredible True Tale of Disaster at Sea*; and *Ten Hours Until Dawn: The True Story of Heroism and Tragedy Aboard the* Can Do, which ALA named an Editor's Choice and which *Booklist* praised as "the best story of peril at sea since *The Perfect Storm*." Tougias's more recent books include *So Close to Home: A True Story of an American Family's Fight for Survival During World War II*; *Overboard!: A True Blue-Water Odyssey of Disaster and Survival*; *Rescue of the Bounty: Disaster and Survival in Superstorm Sandy*; *Derek's Gift: A True Story of Love, Courage and Lessons Learned*; and *The Cringe Chronicles: Mortifying Misadventures with My Dad* (cowritten with his daughter, Kristin Tougias). A frequent lecturer on his work, Tougias lives in Plymouth, Massachusetts.